Final Exit

The practicalities of self-deliverance and assisted suicide for the dying

Derek Humphry

A Dell Trade Paperback

High Praise for
FINAL EXIT

"No decent human being would allow an animal to suffer without putting it out of its misery. It is only to human beings that human beings are so cruel as to allow them to live on in pain, in hopelessness, in living death, without moving a muscle to help them. It is against such attitudes that this book fights."
—Isaac Asimov (author)

"Worldwide, the death rate is one per person. *Final Exit* gives us some important options to this inevitable event."
—Richard D. Lamm (Governor)

"Some people want to eke out every second of life—no matter how grim—and that is their right. But others do not. And that should be *their* right. Until it is, until there is a law which would allow physicians to help people who want a final exit, here is Derek Humphry's book, fittingly named, to guide them."
—Betty Rollin (author, *Last Wish*)

"Nobody else could have done this book. It's the first of its kind in America. People in both the present and future will be in Derek Humphry's debt."
—Dr. Joseph F. Fletcher (theologian)

"Derek Humphry has condensed fifteen years of exploring the issue of euthanasia in an honest, clear, compelling book for those who seek the knowledge that will assure them a good way through this final passage, should it become necessary."
—Dr. Frederick R. Abrams (physician and ethicist)

"An important indictment of medical practice, legal judgment, and of the culture at large for failing to find a way to protect people against unwanted suffering and lingering death in the company of strangers. . . . This book deserves extensive publicity and consideration for what it means to respect people's choices about dying."
—*American Journal of Law and Medicine*

Other books by Derek Humphry

EUTHANASIA

*Jean's Way
  The Right to Die: Understanding Euthanasia
*Let Me Die Before I Wake
  Dying with Dignity

GENERAL

Because They're Black (Martin Luther King Memorial Prize,
  1972)
Passports and Politics
Police Power and Black People
The Cricket Conspiracy
False Messiah

*Available from Dell

For
Joseph F. Fletcher,
Pioneer

ACKNOWLEDGMENTS

I have been rich in helpers to produce this book. My colleagues at Hemlock, Cheryl K. Smith, Kristin A. Larson, and Michele A. Trepkowski have been constructively critical and supportive. Sound advice has come from Warren Sparks, Gerald A. Larue, David B. Clarke, Pieter Admiraal, and many others. I take responsibility for all errors and opinions within.

AUTHOR'S NOTE

As many of the readers of this book will be people with poor sight, it has been set in large type to assist them. Also, this book assumes the reader's ethical acceptance of the right to choose to die when terminally ill and thus the arguments for and against are not addressed. The history and controversy of this issue can be found in *The Right to Die: Understanding Euthanasia* and *Dying with Dignity*.

Darkling I listen; and, for many a time
I have been half in love with easeful Death,
Call'd him soft names in many a mused rhyme,
To take into the air my quiet breath;
Now more than ever seems it rich to die,
To cease upon the midnight with no pain . . .

John Keats
1795–1821

CONTENTS

Part 1

Self-Deliverance
for the
Dying Person

Part 2

Euthanasia Involving
Doctors and Nurses

Introduction to the Paperback Edition

This book caused a sensation in North America when it appeared in hardcover in 1991. The nerve to actually give dying people printed guidance on how to end their lives if their suffering was unbearable!

It is all right to send young people into killing wars, to judicially execute murderers, to be entertained in movies and on television by a staggering stream of murder and brutality. But show compassion to the terminally ill who might want to check out? Leaders of the medical and legal professions threw up their hands in horror; a Roman Catholic church leader called it "a new low in publishing."

But *Final Exit* lifted the hypocritical stone which had overlain a gray area of our society for years. More than half a million people rushed to buy the book. It sold faster than it could be reprinted. There was no advertising, no paid promotion, no organized hype. Yet at one point in 1991 it was the best-selling nonfiction hardcover book in America, and for eighteen weeks it topped the *New York Times* best-seller list in its category. During 1992 it was published in every major language in the world.

Why?

We are all going to die—the later the better, of course. Most people want control and choice over what happens to their bodies. The majority of deaths are peaceful and painless but a few are not. Occasionally a lingering death, destroying the quality of life, is unendurable. Who will be the unlucky ones? At book-signing sessions last year some individuals commented to me: "This is the best insurance policy I've ever bought."

I hope you, the reader, will never actually need to use the information in this book. But you might.

Increasingly physicians and nurses are being asked by patients for euthanasia—help with a good death. Whether and how these requests should be met by health professionals is addressed in the second half of the book.

CAUTION
If you are thinking of ending your life because you are depressed, or cannot cope with the pressures of this difficult world, do not use this book. It is for dying individuals who need such information and will find it a great solace.

I ask people with suicidal thoughts to share them with family or friends and if this does not help to call one of the hot lines or help lines listed in their local telephone book, and presented in Appendix C of this book.

Please respect the true intentions of *Final Exit:* the right of a terminally ill person with unbearable suffering to know how to choose to die.

—**Derek Humphry**
April 1992

Introduction

When my first wife could no longer bear the pain and deterioration of her body and the distressed quality of her life from cancer, she asked me to help her end her life. It was both a logical and a poignant request.

But what should I do? I was not a doctor or a pharmacist. Violent ending of life, such as shooting, stabbing, or strangling, was deeply abhorrent to me, largely because my thirty-five years as a newspaper reporter had too often shown me the ugly end results.

"Find a doctor who will give us a lethal overdose that I can take," Jean pleaded. Unable to bear to see her suffering and noting the calmness of her request, I decided, then and there, to help.

Who could I ask? The three doctors who had been treating her with great skill and dedication came to mind first. They had spent so much time caring for her, although they now recognized—and spoke openly to her and to me—that death was approaching, and that they were running out of countermeasures.

However, I was thinking of asking one of these three highly professional men to commit a crime: that of assisting a suicide. The penal code takes no account of a person's wish to die, nor of how close and inevitable death may be. If it were discovered that one of them had helped my wife to die, that individual would be subject to prosecution in court, and disqualification from practicing medicine.

I couldn't ask them, I decided. But I still had to help Jean—she was depending on me.

Then I remembered a young doctor whom I had met many years before while reporting on medical matters for my newspaper.

I called "Dr. Joe" and asked if we could meet. He invited me to his consulting rooms, for he had by now become an eminent physician with a lucrative practice. As prestigious and powerful as he was, he still had not lost the compassion and humanity that I had noted in earlier years. I told him how seriously ill Jean was and of her desire to die soon. He questioned me closely about the state of the disease, its effects on her, and what treatments she had undergone.

As soon as he heard that some of her bones were breaking at the slightest sudden movement, he stopped the conversation. "There's no quality of life left for her," he said. He got up from his desk and strode to his medicine cabinet.

Dr. Joe did some mixing of pills, and handed a vial to me. He explained that the capsules should be emptied into a sweet drink to reduce the bitter taste.

"This is strictly between you and me," he said, looking straight into my eyes.

"You have my word that no one will ever know

of your part in this," I promised. I thanked him and left.

A few weeks later, when Jean knew the time had come, she asked me for the drugs. As wrenching as it was, I had to agree. We spent the morning reminiscing about our twenty-two years together. Then, after dissolving the pills in some coffee, we said our last good-byes. I watched as Jean picked up the coffee and drank it down. She barely had time to murmur, "Good-bye, my love," before falling asleep. Fifty minutes later she stopped breathing.

My wife died in 1975 as she wished and as she deserved. However, to accomplish that, two crimes were committed.

First, Dr. Joe broke the law by prescribing drugs for a patient not registered with him, a patient he had never seen. Also, he had assisted a suicide because he handed over the drugs knowing what they were intended for.

Second, I committed the crime of assisting a suicide, the penalty for which in Britain, where I was living at the time, is up to fourteen years imprisonment. (Although this incident happened in England, it could as well have happened in America, where I now live, because the laws in the United States and all Western countries on this issue are almost exactly the same. The penalty in California, for example, is five years.)

Now, did Dr. Joe and I commit truly felonious, culpable crimes and did we deserve punishment? Aren't these archaic laws ready to be changed to situations befitting modern understanding and morality?

Not everybody has as good a friend in the medical profession as I had. Moreover, why should caring doctors like Dr. Joe have to take such appalling risks?

Had I broken down when interviewed by detectives about Jean's death and revealed Dr. Joe's identity, he would have been prosecuted and professionally ruined. There are other cases in which that has happened. Also, there was the hypocrisy of how it all turned out.

The authorities only learned of the manner of Jean's death from my 1978 biography of her, *Jean's Way.* The book caused such a stir they felt obliged to interrogate me. When the police came to talk to me, I immediately confessed to them and offered to plead guilty at any trial. But, a few months later I received a note from the public prosecutor: he had decided not to charge me.

The taboo on suicide for reasons of health has been broken since 1980. It is now recognized that elder suicide is widespread and, while it may need to be addressed in terms of social and health care policy, it does not deserve spontaneous condemnation. There is evidence of considerable public—and legal—sympathy for mercy killers, those desperate people who unilaterally kill their loved ones in the belief that it is the only compassionate thing to do. Intellectual giants such as Arthur Koestler and Bruno Bettelheim recently chose to end their lives and did not meet the storm of shock and criticism occasioned by Pitney Van Dusen, the theologian, after his self-deliverance from terminal old age in 1975.

When Dr. Jack Kevorkian chose in 1990 to help Janet Adkins commit suicide in the early stages of Alzheimer's disease, despite some criticism by a few psychologists and self-styled ethicists, there was tremendous public support evidenced for his compassion.

The time is not far off when physician-assisted suicide in justifiable cases will be lawful in enlightened countries. The euthanasia societies in the Netherlands, Britain, France, and the United States are currently finding their law reform proposals much more acceptable to the public, the medical and legal professionals, and the politicians. The Hemlock movement in America has made significant political progress on the West Coast, particularly in the states of Washington and California.

I first published my book on self-deliverance, *Let Me Die Before I Wake*, independently in 1981. No mainstream publisher would touch it. Despite a hail of criticisms and hypocritical commentary, it sold well (more than 130,000 copies) and countless hundreds of people have used it as an informational aid to end lives which, for medical reasons, were unbearable to them. There may have been abuse of the book—when a product is available to some 300 million people in North America, nobody can verify the reasons for every death —but misuse has yet to be documented. In its updated version, *Let Me Die Before I Wake* continues to find readers because it deals with self-deliverance as it affects the individual and the family. In that respect it is timeless.

Now is the time to go one step further. *Final Exit: The Practicalities of Self-deliverance and Assisted Suicide for the Dying* is a book for the 1990s. As a society we have moved on. People today are remarkably well informed about medical problems through television, magazines, and books. Personal autonomy concerning one's bodily integrity has taken hold in the public imagination. Most people have an opinion regarding the situations of Nancy Cruzan, Karen Ann Quinlan, Roswell Gilbert, and other right-to-die celebrity cases. Physicians are now more likely to be seen as "friendly body technicians" and no longer as the rulers of one's bodily health whose every piece of advice must be interpreted as a command.

Final Exit is aimed at helping the public and the health professional achieve death with dignity for those who desire to plan for it.

—**Derek Humphry**
Eugene, Oregon
December 1990

Foreword

My mother had ovarian cancer and she was dying—in her view, not fast enough. On a day I'll never forget I visited her and she made her wishes clear: "I've had a wonderful life, but now it's over, or it should be. I'm not afraid to die, but I am afraid of this illness, what it's doing to me. . . . There's never any relief from it now. Nothing but nausea and this pain. . . . There won't be any more chemotherapy. There's no treatment anymore. So what happens to me now? I know what happens. I'll die slowly. . . . I don't want that. . . . Who does it benefit if I die slowly? If it benefits my children I'd be willing. But it's not going to do you any good. It's not going to do Ed [my husband] any good. There's no point in a slow death, none. I've never liked doing things with no point. I've got to end this."

In my book, *Last Wish*, which is about my mother's fight to die, I describe how difficult that fight was, how if you're very sick—so sick you can hardly swallow—and if you're not prone to violence, it can be very hard to die decently. Decently, meaning quietly and painlessly, with one's family nearby. My mother was lucky. She woke up one day able to swallow and, with my research help, she knew what pills to swallow and she took the pills and peacefully, gracefully, and gratefully, she died. But she almost waited too long. "I get it," she said at one point when she couldn't keep a sip of water down, let alone thirty pills, "I can't die until I feel better."

I loved my mother and do still. I did not want her to die. No matter how natural it is for a parent to die, I found the thought of my mother's absence from life—my life—almost unthinkable. My mother hadn't wanted to die, either. When she was first diagnosed with cancer, she submitted to a year of the most punishing chemotherapy. When the cancer recurred she opted for more of the same. But her body gave out and the doctors—not she—said No more. At that point she had a life that, to her, had effectively ended. As usual, she expressed this with total down-to-earth clarity: "To me this isn't life. Life is taking a walk, visiting my children, eating! Remember how I loved to eat? The thought of food makes me sick now. . . . If I had life I'd want it. I don't want this."

My mother was naive enough to think that once she made this decision—a decision that, in her view, was rational and reasonable, she would, somehow, be able to die. She turned out to be right. For my mother, life had become a trap, an imprisonment, and she managed to escape, but she almost didn't make it. Physician after physician turned down our pleas for help (How many pills? What kind?).

In the seven years since *Last Wish* was published, I've received hundreds of letters. Among the saddest are from people—or the close relatives of people—who have tried to die, failed, and suffered even more. Many of these people sought help—from physicians or family—but were denied it because, although suicide is legal, assisted suicide is not.

It is one of the ironies of modern medicine that technology can now prolong life past its natural span. And once those "miracle machines" are turned on, it is also illegal, most of the time, to turn them off. We are sometimes faced with very tough choices in the name of "progress." So as unnatural as it may seem to take one's own life—some say un-Godly—is it any more natural or Godly to live hooked up to a machine—or in agony—because one's life has been extended by science?

The real question is, does a person have a right to depart from life when he or she is nearing the end and has nothing but horror ahead? And, if necessary, should a physician be permitted to help? Because of what I saw my mother go through, and what I know now about the suffering of others, my answer to those questions is yes.

The medical establishment sometimes makes the point that if pain medication were adequately dispensed, people wouldn't want to die. The fine efforts of hospice notwithstanding, that "if" is one of the biggest I know.

Some people want to eke out every second of life—no matter how grim—and that is their right. But others do not. And that should be *their* right. Until it is, until there is a law which would allow physicians to help people who want a final exit, here is Derek Humphry's book, fittingly named, to guide them.

—**Betty Rollin**

Part 1

Self-deliverance for the Dying Person

CHAPTER ONE

The Most Difficult Decision

This is the scenario: you are terminally ill, all medical treatments acceptable to you have been exhausted, and the suffering in its different forms is unbearable. Because the illness is so serious, you recognize that your life is drawing to a close. Euthanasia comes to mind as a way of release.

The dilemma is awesome. But it has to be faced. Should you battle on, take the pain, endure the indignity, and await the inevitable end which may be weeks, or months, away? Or should you resort to euthanasia, which in its modern language definition has come to mean "help with a good death"?

Today the euthanasia option comes in two ways:

Passive euthanasia. Popularly known as "pulling the plug," the disconnection of life-support equipment without which you cannot live. There is unlikely to be much legal or ethical trouble here so long as you have signed a Living Will and a Durable Power of Attorney for Health Care, documents which express your wishes.

Active euthanasia. Taking steps to end your life, as in suicide, handling the action yourself. Alternatively, and preferably, getting some assistance from another person, which is assisted suicide. (Remember, assisted suicide is still a felony. See Chapter Three.)

If you are not on life-support equipment, then the first option is not available to you because there is no "plug" to pull. Roughly half the people who die in Western society currently are connected to equipment. You may be one of the other half who are not. If you wish to deliberately leave this world, then active euthanasia is your only avenue. Read on, carefully.

(If you consider God the master of your fate, then read no further. Seek the best pain management available and arrange for hospice care.)

If you want personal control and choice over your destiny, it will require forethought, planning, documentation, friends, and decisive, courageous action from you. This book will help, but in the final analysis, whether you bring your life to an abrupt end, and how you achieve this, is entirely your responsibility, ethically and legally.

The task of finding the right drugs, getting someone to help (if you wish that), and carrying out your self-deliverance in a place and in a manner which is not upsetting to other people is your responsibility.

If you have not already done so, sign a Living Will and have it witnessed. Get the one that is valid for your particular state. This document is an advance declaration of your wish not to be connected to life-support equipment if it is adjudged that you are hopelessly and terminally ill.

Or, if you are already on the equipment because of an attempt to save you which failed, a Living Will gives permission for its disconnection. By signing, you are agreeing to take the fatal consequences.

But remember, a Living Will is only a request to a doctor not to be needlessly kept alive on support equipment. It is not an order. It may not be legally enforceable. But as your signed "release," it is a valuable factor in the doctor's thinking about how to handle your dying. The Living Will gives the doctor protection from lawsuits by relatives after your death.

A more potent document is the Durable Power of Attorney for Health Care, which, in different forms, is available in all American states. Here you assign to someone else the power to make health care decisions if and when you cannot.

For example, if your doctor is unable to make you understand the consequences of what treatment is planned then he or she will normally turn to the next of kin. If the next of kin is confused, or has different values, that may not work well.

With the Power of Attorney given to someone in whom you have already confided your general or specific wishes, someone who has accepted the responsibility, then it is most likely that you will get either the kind of treatment—or death—that you desire. A doctor must get the approval of the surrogate you have named. If there is dissent in the family about what to do, the surrogate person (in legal terminology, the "attorney-in-fact") has the final decision. This document is legally enforceable whereas the Living Will is not.

The Durable Power of Attorney for Health Care could be the most significant document you ever sign. As of today, however, it works only for passive euthanasia (the cessation of treatment) and does not empower anybody to perform active euthanasia (helping to die). In deciding the Nancy Cruzan case in 1990, the U.S. Supreme Court gave its official blessing to the Durable Power of Attorney for Health Care as the best way to give clear and convincing evidence of health care wishes.

Since November 1991, the Patient Self-determination Act requires all federally funded hospitals in the United States to advise patients of their right to make out Living Wills.

Undoubtedly the existence of two properly signed advance declarations like those just described will influence people when the question of active euthanasia is considered. It demonstrates that you have gone as far as is legally possible today, and that you have given forethought about the nature of your dying. Membership in the Hemlock Society—or similar organization if you live in another country—is perhaps the most powerful demonstration you can make at present of your beliefs.

A combined Living Will and the Durable Power of Attorney for Health Care can be bought from Hemlock for three dollars plus a self-addressed, fifty-two-cent stamped envelope. There is a guide to completion attached, so you do not necessarily need to employ a lawyer. To be useful, both documents must be distributed beforehand to everybody likely to be concerned with your final hours.

Once these documents are completed, you are ready to tackle the other aspects of bringing your life to an end.

CHAPTER TWO

Shopping for the Right Doctor

If you are interested in the option of euthanasia at life's end, good rapport with your doctor is extremely useful. It is important that your doctor knows your attitude toward dying and death, so that he or she is forewarned. This way there will be one believable witness around who can testify to a rational decision made well before health problems became critical. This may influence possible inquiries by the police or coroner's office.

Therefore, unless you are perfectly satisfied with your present doctor, you should shop around for another.

Have you tested your present doctor's views on right-to-die issues? Don't take any chances. Just because a doctor is a nice person it does not mean the same ethical views as yours are shared. Find out. The perfect opening gambit for dialogue is to arrive at the office with your completed Living Will and Durable Power of Attorney for Health Care. Present these advance declaration documents and candidly ask if they will be respected when the time comes for you to die.

Make your own judgment from the answers you receive as to whether this is the right doctor for you. Do not be influenced by kindly and well-meant remarks such as "Don't worry. I won't let you suffer." Or "Leave it to me. I've never let a patient die in pain." This sort of response is too vague and general to be relied upon.

Pin the doctor down. Would life-support equipment be disconnected once it was realized that there was no hope of recovery? Would such equipment be used regardless of a prognosis of hopeless terminal illness? Having opened the subject with these basic questions, bluntly tell the doctor that you support the Hemlock Society and ask directly if lethal medicines would be supplied to you in certain compassionate, terminal circumstances. The reply to this last question may be an outright rejection, or it may be hedged, because active voluntary euthanasia is not yet lawful and the doctor may be protecting himself or herself. Some doctors who have taken the trouble to think this through will give an outright assurance of help to die in justified and discreet circumstances. But they are still in the minority.

You have to judge from the nature of the answers to your questions whether this is the doctor for you. Of course, if the advance declaration documents are scorned, you must change immediately.

Call your local hospitals and ask for their physician-referral service. If that doesn't work, look up the medical society of your county in the telephone book and ask them. Get the names and numbers of five or six doctors who are reasonably close to you, and also ask for their specialties if you have any particular health problem. Talk to people in your local Hemlock chapter. It is also wise to check with your health insurance company to find out whether these doctors are on their acceptance list. Call ahead and make appointments with these doctors. Say that you would require fifteen or twenty minutes of the doctor's time. You will find that most will appreciate your investigations. For the most part, doctors today are not as stuffy and formal as they used to be.

Speaking for myself, at age 60, I would tend to choose a doctor under 45, male or female, in general preference to an older one. My observation of hundreds of doctors, both in my journalistic and right-to-die careers, is that younger physicians are less dogmatic and self-opinionated. They are more open to new ideas, and better versed in today's medical controversies, including law and ethics, than their elders.

While you are waiting to see the doctor for this selection interview, assess the appearance of the waiting room and whether the magazines are changed regularly. Are the staff pleasant and helpful? Here are clues to the level of consideration given to the patient. You do not want a doctor who is just running a business! If you are kept waiting some time, observe whether the doctor apologizes for the delay and at least hints at the reason why.

Be quick to put the doctor at ease. You do the talking. Tell who you are, where you live, and what your health priorities will be. Be candid about why you are changing doctors; it might only be that you have changed residence. Briefly describe any medical problem you have. After getting responses, bring up the Living Will matter followed by the more testing issue of helping to die.

Don't be nervous about asking your doctor for some objective criteria. Where did qualification as a physician take place and when? At which hospital or hospitals does the doctor have privileges? Is this doctor a board-certified specialist? It is very important to ask what arrangements can be made for your medical records to be transferred from your old doctor to a new one. There is no national law in the United States covering privately held medical records but most states grant the patient or patient's representative the right to examine and copy their medical records. There may be restrictions or exemptions when the information is considered harmful to the patient, especially with mental health records. Most states insist that one doctor give them to another when requested in writing to do so by the patient. Doctors may refuse to do so when a bill has been left unpaid. Usually there will be no trouble about transfer of records, but should there be, ask your state health department or attorney for help.

Do not sign up with any doctor on the spot. Go home and think about your research. Of course, if you have a spouse or companion, it is preferable that you make these doctor-shopping visits together. When one of you is ill, it is often the companion who must communicate a great deal with the doctor. Share your thoughts about the various doctors before coming to a decision.

When you have made your choice, find out which hospital that doctor most uses for admitting patients. This hospital might have a preadmission procedure. Some even promote this feature with tours of the facilities and free lunches. If possible, get copies of your Living Will and Durable Power of Attorney for Health Care lodged with the hospital in advance. (You will by now have deposited them with your doctor.) If your record has no activity, this could be lost or filed away forgotten, so it is a wise precaution to take it with you on the first admission, if possible.

Until tested by serious problems, you cannot make a perfect assessment of which doctor is the best for you. All you can do while "shopping around" is to check if you can communicate well with this person. But that is a big start.

CHAPTER THREE

Beware of the Law

Helping another person to die is presently against the law. You may think this a stupid, unreasonable ban, but we live in a society under the rule of law so we have to be careful about what we do. Hopefully the time is not far off when the law will be modified to permit physician aid-in-dying, but we are not there yet.

Only one country presently permits a doctor to help a patient to die by request—the Netherlands. Dutch doctors have been helping suffering people to accelerate their end since 1973 when a seminal court case laid down the standards by which this could be done. But it is no good thinking of going to the Netherlands—also known as Holland—because they have an absolute rule against euthanasia for foreigners.

The basis for this rule is that the doctor must know the patient well. Also, the family has to be informed, which is certainly sound thinking. But I believe the real reason is that the Dutch just don't want the world's terminal illness problems dumped on them—they have their own fair share. They also do not want to gain an unsavory reputation by being labeled a suicide center. I agree.

Every country should solve its own problems, although we can learn a great deal from the Dutch experience.

Suicide, however, is not a crime, nor is attempted suicide. In many places it was, but it has not been prosecuted in this country and others since the 1960s. Mentally ill people who are suicidal can be held in confinement for short periods for their own protection, but that is a civil, not criminal, law.

It is against the law everywhere to assist a suicide—no matter what the reason. It is no answer legally to say that this was what the person wanted or that it was an act of extreme compassion. About half the states of the United States have laws which specifically prohibit assisted suicide, but even if a state does not have such a law on its books, that does not mean it is permissible. The state may bring charges under a more general law, such as manslaughter or murder. Bertram Harper found this out to his cost when he flew with his terminally ill wife from California to Michigan in the summer of 1990 thinking he would be able to help her die without fear of prosecution. Mrs. Harper died in a motel room in Detroit in the presence of her husband and daughter, as she had wanted. The next day Mr. Harper was charged with first-degree murder.

Yet hundreds of people in America still do help their loved ones to die every year. About one helper a year is threatened by the authorities with prosecution; about one person every two years lands in court. In the majority of these cases these individuals have chosen to make their action public to make a campaigning point. They deliberately gave themselves away. But Mr. Harper spoke to Detroit police in the naive belief that he had committed no crime for which he could be charged.

If you are asked by a loved one to assist in death, consider the following:

1. In terms of personal philosophy, and your relationship to this person, is it the right thing to do?

2. Who else knows, or might get to know, about this, and will they keep it a secret?

3. If the law enforcement authorities find out, are you prepared to take the consequences, whatever they may be?

In my opinion, before assenting to assist, the answers to questions one and three must be an unequivocal YES, while the answer to two is a matter of personal judgment.

What does "assisting" mean in this context?

Assisting in dying could simply mean being present during the happening and giving love and moral support to the act. There is no illegality in that. You cannot be accused in court of merely being present at a suicide. Being part of this act is really the most fundamental part of the Hemlock Society credo: a dying person should not have to do it alone. Isolation at such a time is an inhuman experience.

Never join in the slightest attempt to persuade

a dying person to end life. Rather, argue gently against such action, seeking alternatives, testing the will of the patient. Many laws are specific about the criminality of "counseling and procuring" a suicide. In any event, it is ethically a wrong thing to do.

Providing information about how dying persons may end life is not a crime, at least in the United States. It may be in Britain where EXIT, the English euthanasia group, in 1983 had to withdraw its *Guide to Self-deliverance.* Hemlock, however, has never been prosecuted in the United States—nor threatened with prosecution—for *Let Me Die Before I Wake* or its drug dosage charts.

Actually supplying the means—drugs, plastic bag, elastic bands, etc.—may well be a crime, although there are no clear court examples to confirm that it is so. What authorities will look for is evidence of intent. Hemlock is very careful about keeping clear of this. Individuals must personally act with caution and discretion.

Touching the person in the act of helping is where criminal liability is possible. Giving an injection, holding the cup to mouth, helping to put the plastic bag over the head and securing it—all are actions which prosecutors could use to enforce the laws against assistance in dying.

In order to avoid possible trouble here are some basic rules:

1. Don't persuade the dying person; rather it is advisable to try up to a point to dissuade.

2. Don't touch. It must be self-deliverance.

3. If you must touch because the patient is physically helpless—amyotrophic lateral sclerosis (ALS) might be the most common example—absolute discretion before and after the action is paramount.

4. Give comfort and love, and provide privacy and security.

5. Make sure that the person you are helping has left a note giving the reasons for this action and accepting personal responsibility.

6. Before and afterward, say nothing to anybody. If the police should ask questions, do not speak except in the presence of a lawyer. Do not assume you are in the clear; that has trapped many people. Should you be subsequently asked questions by anybody, state emphatically that you gave the dead person no encouragement, you did not touch, and were merely present as an observer because you enjoyed a close relationship.

Law exists to prevent abuse. If your assistance in helping to ease the suffering of a dying person who could bear no more was a loving act, and justifiable in human terms, then your conscience is clear.

". . . The rest is silence," as Hamlet said as he died.

* * * * *

I cannot emphasize strongly enough that people (doctors included) should only help each other to die if there is a bonding of love or friendship, and mutual respect. If the association is anything less, stand aside. This is too serious a matter to be relegated to a poor, a casual, or a brief relationship.

CHAPTER FOUR

The Hospice Option

"Don't consider euthanasia," a friend might reasonably say, "think about hospice." Certainly.

There are two types of hospice: inpatient and home hospice. In America you are unlikely to be offered a bed in a hospice facility since there are very few. In Britain and France, a bed is a distinct possibility in difficult cases. Because of population size, distance, and financing problems, the United States has had to go with home hospice. There, however, are some good ones.

The most precious service hospice offers is respite from the burden of care for a family member or members looking after a dying person. Hospice may be able to provide someone for several days, nights, or a week to enable a stressed-out caregiver to take a break. Hospice doctors, who are especially skilled in pain management, make house calls.

Essentially, all we are speaking about here is good medical care for the dying. It is interesting to note that Scandinavian countries do not permit hospice to even start up; for them good home care is part of the total medical package provided by their doctors and nurses.

Inpatient hospices, where they are available, provide exceptionally skilled nursing care and pain management in a loving environment freed from many of the customary restrictions surrounding normal hospitals. To enter a hospice you —or your family—must agree that death is the certain outcome of your illness, and that you seek care, not treatment. There will be no life-support equipment, such as respirators or artificial feeding, available.

Neither will you be helped to die in any deliberate manner. A hospice undertakes to do everything within its power to relieve suffering but makes no guarantees. It all depends on what you mean by suffering. That comes in many forms to various people.

Some hospices are run by religious orders or individuals. Others are organized out of humanitarian motives and have little or no religious affiliation. The first thing to check is whether your ethical beliefs are the same as those of the hospice. There might be an embarrassing confrontation at prayer time!

Whether or not you wish to die in hospice care —assuming there is one in your district—comes down to how your terminal illness is being coped with, by you and your family. You must also decide whether or not you wish to put yourself into their hands and tough it out to the end, or whether you want to keep open the option of accelerated death should suffering become unbearable.

There has always been a friendly alliance between many hospices in America and Hemlock. A considerable number of Hemlock members also work as volunteers in hospice. One leading Hemlock member in California was for some years chairperson of her local hospice.

This liaison has always been strongest on the West Coast. From what I have observed this is probably because hospice groups there are more likely to be in the hands of people with purely humanitarian motives. On the East Coast hospices are more likely—but not exclusively—to be founded by religious people.

Sometimes hospice staff call Hemlock and report that a patient of theirs is asking about euthanasia. We are asked to send out literature directly to this person. On the other hand, Hemlock members in distress sometimes call our headquarters and request the name of the nearest hospice. A geographical guide is maintained for this purpose.

Many hospice adherents believe that it is only fear of pain that drives people to ask for euthanasia. They repeat the statements of England's Dr. Cecily Saunders, the founder of modern hospice techniques, that euthanasia is completely unnecessary now that sophisticated drug administration can control most pain.

Dame Cecily and other experts agree that there is about 10 percent of terminal pain that cannot be controlled. This leaves a lot of people still suffering.

More importantly, it is not just pain, or fear of

it, that drives people into the arms of the euthanasia movement. It is the symptoms of an illness, and often the side effects of medication, that damage the quality of people's lives. To take admittedly extreme examples, a person may not wish to live with throat cancer after the tongue has been removed and the face disfigured; or, with abdominal cancer, to be unable to walk across a room without evacuating their bowel. If reading or watching television is the great comfort of life, loss of sight is a tremendous blow if added to the knowledge that death is impending.

Quality of life, personal dignity, self-control, and above all, choice, are what both hospice and the euthanasia movement are concerned with. It is the element of personally deciding when and how to die which hospice cannot support. It is too intimate, too individual.

Both hospice and euthanasia provide valuable services to different types of people with varying problems.

* * * * *

For information about hospice services, write or call:

National Hospice Organization
1901 North Moore Street, Suite 901
Arlington, VA 22209
(703) 243-5900

CHAPTER FIVE

The Cyanide Enigma

Is death by ingestion of cyanide the best means of self-deliverance? Is it as fast as in the James Bond movies—twelve seconds?

How much pain does cyanide induce? Does it always work? These questions come at me all the time.

Some of the most famous suicides in modern history have been by cyanide. Hermann Göring escaped the gallows at Nuremberg in 1945 by biting on a glass vial of cyanide within a brass bullet which had been smuggled into his cell. Wallace Carothers, the inventor of nylon, who had a doctorate in organic chemistry, committed suicide in a hotel room in Philadelphia in 1937 by drinking potassium cyanide in lemon juice.

Perhaps the world's most unrecognized genius, Alan Turing, who designed the theory behind the computer in the 1930s, took his life in 1954 while under personal stress. Like Snow White, he bit into a poisoned apple dipped in witches brew. But, unlike the fairy tale, Turing had dipped his fruit in a jar of potassium cyanide solution and there could be no awakening by a prince's kiss.

About 800 of the 913 people who died in Jonestown, Guyana, in 1978, took potassium cyanide that had been put into a soft drink. The adults drank from cups; many of the children had it squirted down their throats by syringes.

In what I consider to be the most reliable of all the accounts of the tragedy, San Francisco journalist Tim Reiterman, who was wounded in the shooting event that preceded the mass suicide and murders, reported that "parents and grandparents cried hysterically as their children died—not quickly and not painlessly. The doomed convulsed and gagged as the poison took effect. For several minutes they vomited, they screamed, they bled." (*Raven: The Untold Story of the Rev. Jim Jones and His People,* Dutton, New York, 1982.)

We do not know whether Göring, Turing, and Carothers suffered pain or not. That is the dilemma of death by cyanide—it is usually a lonely act. Remarkably few who make the attempt live to tell the tale. It seems clear, however, that there was considerable suffering by those who died in Jonestown.

Even in some well-planned suicides by cyanide, death is not always certain. In 1987 two terrorists being questioned in Bahrain in connection with the bombing of a jet airliner, bit on cyanide pills contained within cigarettes. "Just after swallowing the pills, they both fell to the floor and their bodies went very stiff," an eyewitness said. The man died four hours later; the woman terrorist recovered to stand trial.

During an arrest in connection with the murder

of twenty-five people in northern California in 1985, a suspect bit on one of several cyanide pills in his possession. He died four days later in the hospital.

Clearly, experts feel it is the most effective method of self-destruction: more than 40 percent of the suicides among chemists, both men and women, occur from swallowing cyanide, according to a report in *The New York Times* (8/4/87).

This account was given to me by the son of a chemist in New Jersey: "After his retirement, when he was thinking about ending his life as his prostate cancer advanced, my father went to a chemical supply house and purchased a bottle of about twelve ounces of ferrocyanide, and a few other related chemicals so as not to arouse suspicion. He was very forthright and open about this with his family. On the bottle of ferrocyanide he wrote: 'This is my control.' About six months later he dissolved a teaspoonful in half a glass of water and added a little vinegar to help release the cyanide gas, even though the natural acid in the stomach is probably sufficient. He died in my mother's arms after two breaths and no indication of pain or violence."

A doctor tells me of a friend of his, a university professor, who prepared a cyanide capsule which he took with a glass of strong lemonade, and was found dead the next day, sitting in his easy chair in a relaxed attitude.

A rare eyewitness account appeared in the London newspaper, *Today* (9/16/87), in which a 27-

year-old woman, severely crippled in a road accident, elected to end her life by sipping cyanide and water through a straw. A woman friend who was present took a photograph and made a recording of her wish to die. A peaceful death occurred thirteen seconds after the drink was consumed, according to the report.

Contrast this with the view of a doctor friend of mine who says he has had direct knowledge of a suicide by cyanide which was "miserable and violent, marked by frequent tetanic convulsions while awake. It was painful in the extreme. I would absolutely not recommend it."

Other doctors I talked to about cyanide referred to the lack of medical knowledge on the subject. All had an impression that although it was quick it was also painful. They would only use it themselves as a very last resort.

Those states of the United States that have used gas chambers to judicially execute murderers give us some knowledge of the effect of hydrogen cyanide (HCN). Unconsciousness is instant with death following in five to ten minutes, although accounts vary. Some states use a massive infusion of drugs directly into the veins of the prisoner who is strapped to a gurney. First, sodium thiopental is used to put the condemned individual to sleep; then follows pavulon, a muscle relaxant similar to the South American poison, curare, together with potassium chloride to stop the heart.

From reports, it seems that consciousness is lost almost immediately and death follows within ten minutes. Doctors and nurses have always refused —and have been supported in this by their professional organizations—to participate in executions. This is understandable, but may have resulted in some problems when an untrained person has not found the vein properly and the needle slipped out.

In the Netherlands, where assisted suicide has been widely practiced with the consent of the courts for nearly twenty years, doctors will not even consider cyanide, although a significant number of patients elect to drink a poison themselves. Physicians have concocted other potions which they consider superior; this will be explained in another chapter. Whether their dismissal stems from a prejudice against cyanide as the infamous chosen means of exit by emotionally suicidal people, or from scientific judgment, is hard to assess. The world's leading expert on practical euthanasia, Dr. Pieter V. Admiraal, who lives in the Netherlands, and is the author of a booklet, *Justifiable Euthanasia: A Guide to Physicians*, tells me: "I have no experience with cyanide. Rumor tells me that it's cruel to see . . . cramps and vomiting . . . with many minutes of awareness."

The textbooks tell us that hydrocyanic acid and its sodium and potassium salts are about the most potent and swift-acting poisons known to man. There is cyanide present in many rodenticides and in the seeds of most common fruits, notably cherries, plums, and apricots. Cyanide comes in different forms: hydrocyanic acid, nitroprusside, potassium cyanide, and sodium cyanide. Another name for it is prussic acid. The compounds of cyanide have wide industrial applications: electroplating, ore-extracting processes, photography, polishing metals, and the fumigation of warehouses and ships. Death can come from inhalation of a mere 50mg of the acid while between 200 to 300mg of the potassium or sodium salt is fatally toxic.

"If large amounts have been absorbed, collapse is usually instantaneous, the patient falling unconscious, often with a loud cry and dying almost immediately. This is known as the 'apoplectic form' of cyanide poisoning." (*Poisoning: Toxicology, Symptoms, Treatments,* by Jay M. Arena and Charles C. Thomas, Illinois.) Most of the textbooks speak of "convulsions, coma, and death within five minutes" in connection with cyanide. News reports and textbooks of suicides almost always speak of the strong smell of almonds and foam on the victim's mouth.

"If the stomach is empty and free gastric acidity is high, poisoning is especially fast. After large doses, some victims have had time only for a warning cry before sudden loss of consciousness." (*Clinical Toxicology of Commercial Products. Acute Poisoning.* Gosselin, Hodge, Smith, and Gleason. 4th edition. Williams and Wilkins, Baltimore and London.)

The Nazis murdered millions of Jews, Gypsies, homosexuals, political dissidents, and mentally and physically handicapped people in Germany between 1940 and 1945 mainly by use of cyanide acid gas, which they called Zyklon B. While the Nazi motives were barbarous, ruthless, and unforgivable, the actual deaths were swift, though this is small consolation to the families of the killed. The post-war Nuremberg trials and other hearings meted out justice to the Nazi criminals. For their part in the so-called "mercy euthanasias" of the handicapped, four doctors were hanged at Nuremberg and five others sentenced to life imprisonment. Others were caught and tried later. It was a failure by a section of the medical profession that must never be allowed to happen again.

In the 1980s, the situation with regard to the suffering of terminally ill people was as tragic in Germany as elsewhere. Regardless of the terrible connotation given to the word "euthanasia" (which means help with a good death) by the Nazi atrocities, some people felt that compassionate action to help the dying was needed. In 1980, a pro-euthanasia society was formed, *Deutsche Gesellschaft für Humanes Sterben* (German Society for Humane Dying), by a small group of brave people under the leadership of Hans Henning Atrott.

Unlike groups in other countries, DGHS found it did not need to campaign for a change in the law on assisted suicide. There was no legal prohibition on helping another to die in justified circumstances so long as the request for help was clear and convincing. When tested by Professor

Hackethal, who openly helped a cancer victim to die in 1983, although some authorities wished to prosecute him, the law protected Hackethal, as it did others who later followed his example.

The German euthanasia society, which has a large membership and numerous chapters, has worked for public acceptance of voluntary, justified euthanasia for the terminally ill in today's world. It views the Nazi atrocities of fifty years ago as a never-to-be-forgotten piece of history though still not an event which should prevent compassion for today's dying people who suffer.

Hans Atrott has written to me that he knows of more than 300 people who have ended their lives with the use of cyanide to avoid further suffering. He has been present at several cases. His organization believes this is by far the best method — though it has to be done with a certain sophistication.

Atrott says that correctly used, death by cyanide is by no means violent. It is quick and gentle. "Anybody who saw a correctly applied cyanide self-deliverance would want it for himself or herself," he claims. He blames cyanide's bad name on the failure in medical literature to distinguish between the properties of hydrogen cyanide (HCN) and potassium cyanide (KCN) and their differing usefulness.

DGHS has learned both from medical scientists and experience that KCN alone is the useful agent in suicide. That is borne out by the stories I have researched elsewhere in the world. The recommended technique by DGHS is:

1. Take a small glass of cold tap water. (Not mineral water, nor any sort of juice or soda water because of its acidity.)

2. Stir one gram, or 1.5g at most, of KCN (potassium cyanide) into the water. (To use more than this amount would cause burning of the throat.)

3. After about five minutes the KCN is dissolved and ready to drink. It remains drinkable for several hours, but not more.

4. Once the potion is drunk, consciousness will be lost in about a minute. There will be just time to rinse out the glass (to ensure that no one else accidentally drinks from it) and lie down. But beware—a person extremely weakened by illness might black out in twenty seconds.

5. While in the coma, death will follow in fifteen minutes or at most forty-five minutes, depending on the physical strength of the person and whether the stomach is full or empty. An empty stomach promotes faster death.

6. During the coma period, the dying person will breathe heavily or snore, similar to people who have taken a lethal overdose of barbiturates.

Atrott notes that with a person who is seriously terminally ill, death is so peaceful that often doctors do not detect suicide, and sign the death certificate as being from natural causes. Of course, an autopsy would uncover this. The simple cleverness of the DGHS method is that while the person ingests potassium cyanide, the effect of the water is to turn it into hydrogen cyanide. This is borne out by evidence in textbooks that flocks of sheep that have eaten plants containing cyanide do not die—so long as they drink no water. If they are near water, they inevitably die.

Obtaining potassium cyanide is easy for people working in chemistry or industry who know the sources, and have cause to purchase it. However, it is difficult to secure by others because its lethality is notorious. From all the evidence it appears to me to be viable for self-deliverance from a terminal illness—when used with the greatest of care. Misused, death from cyanide can be painful in the extreme, violent in fact. No caring person would want loved ones or friends to witness such a shocking experience. I remain skeptical about peaceful death from any form of cyanide.

CHAPTER SIX

Death—Hollywood Style?

In the years since Hemlock was formed in 1980, my most persistent question from callers and letter writers has been whether graceful and pain-free self-deliverance can be achieved by the injection of air into a vein. The aesthetic attractiveness of this antiseptic method of accelerated death—apparently clean, bloodless, clinical, swift, and painless—obviously fascinates many people.

Detective story writers—notably Dorothy L. Sayers—have glamorized it ever since that literary genre first flourished in the 1920s. Whenever a Hollywood movie calls for a suicide, the air bubble method is favored by directors. In *Coming Home*, for instance, the 1978 film about veterans returning from the Vietnam war, that starred Jane Fonda and Jon Voight, a man is fleetingly seen committing suicide by an injection of air from a syringe.

A segment of the television hospital drama series, *St. Elsewhere*, shows a young man killing himself by this means. "It looked so nice and easy," a Hemlock member wrote to me. "Is it really?"

A review of available medical literature shows only one case of it actually happening, and that instance has ambiguous features. In 1949 Dr. Herman Sander, a New Hampshire general practitioner, injected 40cc's of air into the veins of a cancer patient, Mrs. Abbie Burotto, age 59. She was in the final stages of her terminal illness. Unwisely, Dr. Sander entered into the hospital records the statement: "Patient given ten cc's of air intravenously, repeated three times. Expired ten minutes after this was started."

A person at the hospital who maintained records saw this unusual entry and reported it to her superiors. Dr. Sander was immediately arrested.

The case became a *cause célèbre* in euthanasia and aroused enormous public attention, much of it supportive of Dr. Sander. At his trial in 1950, Dr. Sander pleaded "not guilty" to first-degree murder and denied that his injection of air caused the patient's death. One physician testified that he could find no pulse during an examination on the morning of Mrs. Burotto's death, and that she might have expired before Dr. Sander gave the injection. A nurse also said that she thought the woman was dead before both doctors saw her.

Although found not guilty of any crime, Dr. Sander had his license to practice medicine revoked. There was a public outcry and it was later reinstated. It was reported that his medical practice increased substantially.

Does it work? Is this a practical form of euthanasia for either the patient or a doctor to use?

First, it is probably detectable in an autopsy,

because air bubbles would most likely gather in the right side of the heart. It is assumed by doctors who have given the matter some thought that, while some bubbles may get through to the lungs, the air-embolus in the heart itself prevents anything from going to the lungs.

A professor of anatomy told me: "What it feels like, of course, is impossible to say, because I don't imagine anyone has survived the injection of enough air to fill the heart chambers. Smaller quantities of air would pass through and out to the lungs, and would produce a shut-down of activity in small segments of the lung, probably without much sensation."

Dr. Colin Brewer, a physician and psychiatrist in London, who has studied all forms of euthanasia for twenty years, commented: "As far as I recall from my medical teaching, air embolism certainly causes a rapid death, though whether it is a particularly pleasant one I simply don't know. And since it is exceedingly rare I don't suppose many other people know either. You certainly would have to inject quite a bit of air very quickly, otherwise it is absorbed before the blood has reached the heart. Nurses are usually fanatical about removing the last, minute bubble from anything they inject, but I understand that you need to inject at least twenty cc's, which is an awful lot of bubbles. The air has to be injected into a vein, and I imagine a lot of people will not find this easy to do themselves, especially if they are elderly, since old people's veins tend to be tricky to get into."

Professor Yvon Kenis, an oncologist who is also the head of a Belgian euthanasia society, tells me that in his long career he has never come across any instance, although he was told about the risks in medical school.

"My impression is that this is not a suitable method, nor a gentle death in humans," he said. "Particularly, it would be extremely difficult to utilize as a method of suicide. During the injection, the first part of the air may induce temporary cardiac arrest, and loss of consciousness. This might be reversible, possibly with very serious consequences, such as paralysis or permanent brain damage. I have to stress that this is only an impression and that I have no real scientific information on the subject."

Dr. Admiraal describes the theoretical air bubble method of suicide as impossible, disagreeable, and cruel. "To kill somebody with air you would have to inject at least 100-200ml as quickly as possible in a vein as big as possible close to the heart. You would have to fill the whole heart with air at once. The heart would probably beat on for several minutes, perhaps five to fifteen minutes, and during the first minutes the person may be conscious."

From this it is clear that attempting death from air embolism is most unsatisfactory as a form of self-deliverance or assisted suicide.

CHAPTER SEVEN

Bizarre Ways to Die

I don't really want to write this chapter. But I have to. People write to me almost every day with ideas for self-destruction about which they have heard or have invented themselves. A good deal of my time is spent writing back saying, "No, I don't think so. Not recommended."

A significant section of the public is fascinated by curious and outlandish ways to kill oneself. So I will deal with bizarre suicide here; if I don't my mail will increase significantly from people who feel cheated.

First, let me deal with some truly weird cases of suicide technique.

As the sun rose one day in Seattle in 1986, it triggered a device that shot its inventor. This man, a disturbed and unhappy electronics engineer, had set up a photoelectric cell in the window of his motel room. A wire from the cell ran to a device with elements which he placed on his chest. Sunlight heated the elements, which in turn detonated a firecracker. The explosion of the firecracker released a firing pin which shot a round straight into his heart. I suppose, for a man with his interests, it was "going out in style."

Another depressed man who collected rattle-snakes as a hobby in southern California deliberately allowed one of his pets to bite him five or six times on the right hand. He suffered a fatal heart attack.

For sheer determination, this 1987 story is hard to top. A 22-year-old man in England, who broke up with his girlfriend, threw himself at four different cars and a truck, tried to strangle himself, and jumped out of a window. He was treated in the hospital for minor injuries!

A 23-year-old man in Austria who was suffering from AIDS killed himself by deliberately driving his car into an oncoming railway train. Driving cars into barriers or trees is a frequent method of suicide, undoubtedly made attractive by the hope that it won't be considered as suicide but as an accident. Government statistics show that about 30,000 people in the United States commit suicide each year—by no means the world's highest rate —but experts who have studied suicidal behavior tell me that the true rate is certainly double, and perhaps triple, because so many go undetected.

I am not going to detail methods of suicide by electrocution, hanging, drowning, shooting, gassing, poisonous plants, and domestic cleaning chemicals, because they are all unacceptable to people who believe, as I do, in voluntary euthanasia for the terminally ill. But I will detail their drawbacks and objections.

ELECTROCUTION. Workmen are sometimes killed by electric shock, but some have had miraculous survivals. Sometimes survival from a shock results in serious paralysis and bodily harm. Nowadays most electrical systems are so heavily protected with fuses and cut-out devices that they will short-circuit and cease to transmit current when under strain. Some people tell me that their mode of self-deliverance will be getting into the bath and pulling an electric heater in after them. It might work, and it might not. Remember also that the person who finds you might also be electrocuted. Unless you are an ingenious and accomplished engineer, electricity is definitely not advised for self-deliverance.

HANGING.   Self-destruction by hanging is almost always an act of protest, a desire to shock and hurt someone. Therefore most euthanasists avoid it. However, at least one Hemlock member disagrees with me. "All one needs is about fifteen minutes of undisturbed time, a length of rope . . . no doctor's assistance is needed . . . it is very quick . . . unconscious in seconds and dead in minutes. It is painless." Yet when I asked him if he would allow family or close friends to find him, he said he would not. Even if it is left to a policeman or paramedic to cut down the corpse, I still think this is an unacceptably selfish way to die. I have never heard of a member of a euthanasia society hanging himself or herself.

DROWNING.   Death comes quickly from hypothermia in bitterly cold water. The lower the temperature the faster the end. But there is always the chance of rescue. This manner of death also leaves unanswered questions for survivors: Was it deliberate? Will the body be found? Will there be an extensive search for the body, costly to public funds?

SHOOTING. This is definitely not the exit of choice for believers in euthanasia. I do hear of some who shoot themselves to escape their suffering, often when it is caused by advanced emphysema. Far fewer women shoot themselves than men. In the United States as a whole, between 50 and 60 percent of all suicides are by guns. Reports indicate that the preferred method is to put the gun into the mouth and shoot upward into the brain. Some who have aimed the gun at the temple have missed the vital spot and survived. Some people shoot themselves in the chest, aiming for the heart. But even that method is not error proof. In 1945 as American occupation troops approached his home in Tokyo, General Tojo, Japan's Prime Minister, prepared to shoot himself. He had his doctor make a chalk mark on his chest where his heart was; then, when the troops were at the front door, he fired a .32 Colt into the spot. Although seriously wounded, he had missed the heart and lived to be tried for war crimes. Tojo was hanged three years later. Medical literature reports the case of one man, anxious not to fail, who put a .32 pistol to one temple and a .22 pistol to the other. He fired both guns simultaneously. Not surprisingly, it produced the result he desired.

The larger the gun, the more likely it is to be effective; and a hollow point bullet makes a larger wound. A .22-caliber gun is rarely lethal, and determined individuals who commit suicide using one often have to fire twice. Unquestionably a gun produces a violent and bloody death, but is preferred by many because of its speed, certainty, and painlessness. This method is not favored by the euthanasia movement because it is messy (who cleans up?) and it has to be a lonely act, the opposite of the right-to-die credo, which aims to share the dying experience.

CAR EXHAUSTS.   Self-gassing by letting the car exhaust of an idling engine into the passenger compartment is a chosen way of death for some, particularly elderly couples who want to go together. An ordinary length of hose is fitted snugly over the exhaust vent to reach into a window, which then is sealed. A small, well-sealed garage would obviate the need for a hose but extra attention would have to be paid to the certainty that there was a full tank of gas and that the engine would idle for two or three hours. The chief drawbacks to this method are the possibility of the engine stopping and the high chance of discovery. The length of time it takes to be fatal depends on the density of the gas in each case, but it seems that unconsciousness precedes a peaceful and slow death. Very few believers in euthanasia opt for this form of deliverance because the risk of discovery during the time taken is large. Nevertheless, thousands of people have killed themselves with vehicle exhausts since the automobile became popular in the 1920s.

OVENS.   This is not possible now that natural gas, pumped from the earth, has replaced the old city gas made in retorts, which was both lethal and explosive.

HOUSEHOLD CLEANING AND DRAIN CHEMICALS.   The prospect of death certainly lies under almost every household kitchen sink. Bleach, lye, and drain-cleaning fluids may kill. The manner of death is painful in the extreme and in certain cases rescue is possible. I have heard of people throwing themselves through plate-glass windows in their death agonies after drinking lye.

CHARCOAL COOKING FIRES. People have accidentally died from lighting charcoal fires in tents or in rooms instead of in the open air. Some have luckily been discovered and rescued in time. This is much too uncertain to be risked in euthanasia. Other lives might be endangered if there were to be an explosion. It is amazing how many people actually consider using this method, and I always advise against it.

POISONOUS PLANTS.   A great many people are obsessed with the thought that they can pluck a plant from their garden and bring about their own demise in a natural fashion. My mailbox is full of such inquiries. Yes, the water plant hemlock, foxglove, oleander, and some other plants can be toxic to the point of lethality. But how much is lethal? No one knows, since it depends on the age of the plant, the condition of the person, the content of the stomach, and so forth. What might kill a child—the frequent accident victim—would not kill an adult. Everything I have ever read about death from plant poisoning indicates that it is risky and painful. Symptoms range from nausea and vomiting to cramping and bloody diarrhea. Burned mouths, dizziness, and visual disturbances are other side effects. Reporting on cases of geriatric patients who had deliberately eaten oleander leaves, the *Western Journal of Medicine* (12/89) said patients either died or survived through differences in age, organ health system, oleander species, and in poison preparation. Moreover, while the identification and naming has been a science since the Middle Ages, the toxicity of plants is far from being an exact science. Too much depends on the site of growth and the time of year the plant is cropped. Altogether, I consider poisonous plants as a means of exit far too unreliable and painful. No matter how desperate you are, don't even think about it!

FREEZING. Not so bizarre, and a method for which I have respect, is freezing to death on a mountain. It takes a certain sort of person to wish to die this way: determined, having knowledge of the mountains, and an enduring courage to carry it off. They must be still fit enough to make the journey. A few terminally ill persons I have known have quietly ascended their favorite mountain late in the day and made sure they were above the freezing line for that particular time of year. They used public transport to get there so a parked car was not spotted. Then, wearing light clothing, they sat down in a secluded spot to await the end. Some have said that they intended to take a tranquilizer to hasten the sleep of death. From what we know of hypothermia, they would pass out as the cold reached a certain level and they would die within a few hours. Of course, in a very cold climate there is no need to climb a mountain.

The originators of this idea were the Eskimos, who used ice floes, and the Japanese, who climbed mountains. In Japanese lore, if the person was unfit to climb the mountain, a son had to carry his parent on his back. Remember, though, that the Eskimos practiced this form of euthanasia to remove the elderly so that the tribe could move fast enough across the tundra to hunt for food. The Japanese did it out of poverty. I do not think this same practice occurs with those two groups today, but a few modern believers in euthanasia have adopted the practice as their preferred method of exit.

NONPRESCRIPTION DRUGS. Because people are frustrated at not being able to secure lethal drugs from their doctor, hardly a day goes by without a letter in my mail asking if such-and-such an over-the-counter drug is lethal. Certainly it is possible to commit suicide with some drugs bought at a pharmacy without a doctor's prescription, but the dying will be slow and painful —and perhaps fail. For example, heavy doses of drugs like aspirin will burn the lining of the stomach over several days. The time such drugs take to work will almost certainly mean discovery and an ambulance trip to the hospital. There is also the possibility of permanent brain or physical damage. I cannot stress this advice enough: Do not use nonprescription drugs for self-deliverance. They are a prescription for disaster.

CHAPTER EIGHT

The Dilemma of Quadriplegics

Not many people who are quadriplegics wish to kill themselves. But some do. I am referring here to these few.

There is no more controversial aspect of euthanasia than that involving the handicapped. Merely to mention it causes my critics to refer to me as a Nazi, wanting to get rid of "burdens on society." That is not my wish. I respect the right of that small number of quadriplegics who want—either now or in the future—to have self-deliverance without being preached to and patronized by those on the religious right.

Unlike my other book on methods of self-deliverance, *Let Me Die Before I Wake*, I am not leaning on case histories here. I will, however, make an exception and talk about James Haig, because his story hit me right between the eyes. I was attending a world euthanasia conference in Oxford, England, in 1980 when a young man in a wheelchair came and asked to talk with me privately.

He had been thrown from his motorcycle after colliding with a car and was left, at age 24, paralyzed from the neck down. Restricted use of his right fingers allowed him to operate an electric wheelchair. James struggled for four years to cope with the shock of being changed from an active sportsman and husband and father into an 84-pound quadriplegic. He had been cared for in the best hospitals and received extensive psychological counseling. Accident insurance had provided ample money to live on.

But James would not accept his condition. He divorced his wife against her wishes. He then joined EXIT, the British voluntary euthanasia society, but found that while the organization was sympathetic it could not directly help him. James tried to arrange his self-destruction twice. Once he drove his wheelchair into a river, but got stuck in the mud. A second time, he asked a friend to provide drugs in a motel room, but the friend changed his mind. James Haig's case became so notorious—and moving—that it was reported extensively in the London newspapers.

At that Oxford meeting, James explained his philosophy to me. Despite all the care, love, and money that had been lavished on him, he said he simply could not live in this smashed condition. He wished to die. "Help me to die, Derek," he pleaded. I demurred. "But you helped Jean to die. Then why not me?"

I had narrowly escaped prosecution in 1978 for helping my terminally ill wife to die (see the book, *Jean's Way*, and the play, *Is This the Day?*) and had only just set up the Hemlock Society in America. I explained to James that (1) I was willing to break the law forbidding assistance in suicide for a loved one; and (2) I had launched a highly visible, long-range campaign to educate people in the hope that the law would be reformed to permit physician aid-in-dying for the terminally ill. Therefore to engage in another assistance—to a stranger—clashed with my ethics and could be counterproductive to my reform efforts. I urged him to try to find a person close to him who would help. He was disappointed but I felt we parted on understanding terms.

A few months later I read in the newspapers that James had indeed committed suicide—by setting fire to his house and allowing himself to burn to death. He left a suicide note. I—and probably the numerous other people whom James asked for help—have never forgotten him.

The painfulness of the question of euthanasia for the handicapped is contrasted by the story of Elizabeth Bouvia. In 1983 she decided that her existence since birth paralyzed by cerebral palsy was not worth continuing and checked herself into a California hospital, asking to be allowed to starve herself to death.

The hospital refused to cooperate and went to court seeking to force-feed Elizabeth. (She lost her first case but won the second: you cannot be force fed in California.) A television clip of the court proceedings showed her determinedly asking to be allowed to die by starvation. The case developed into an international media circus and Elizabeth got all the attention she had obviously been craving. There was talk of a book and movie about her life. All this must have caused her to change her mind, because in early 1992 she is still alive and well cared for in a Los Angeles hospital.

For every case I could quote of handicapped people changing their minds, I could cite another where they did not, and went through with their self-deliverance. I meet severely handicapped people at Hemlock gatherings and—to summarize their views—they tell me that they want the option of euthanasia as an insurance against the physical deterioration and sapping illnesses that so often come from enforced inactivity. Some who I knew in the early 1980s are now dead by their own hand; others are still enjoying life.

The real dilemma of the quadriplegic is—as James Haig's story so poignantly illustrates—how to end it alone. It is nearly impossible to carry it out. Hemlock files contain heartrending stories of loved ones suffocating, shooting, cutting the throat, and supplying lethal drugs to handicapped people who desire suicide. Court cases and often imprisonment follows. This letter from a female Hemlock member describes the problem first-hand and better than I can:

"Three years ago I was in a car accident which left me paralyzed from the shoulders down. Though I had a Living Will, I did not have it present at the scene of the accident. I woke up in the Intensive Care Unit on a respirator at a trauma center, with a broken neck, punctured lungs, and a room full of monitors. By the time I became aware of my condition, there was no way that I could request to be taken off the respirator.

"My mind is extremely sharp and I am fully aware, but my quality of life has been reduced to a mere existence. I can do nothing for myself. There is nothing I would like more than to be able to find someone to assist me in self-deliverance because I will never be happy with this lack of quality of life. However, it is impossible to find this type of assistance without some legislation or a friend in the medical field unafraid of the legal ramifications.

"I feel so trapped and utterly hopeless in this situation and have nowhere to turn. Life has no dignity and I feel as though I am sitting here waiting to die. . . . A life without quality and dignity is every bit as bad, if not worse, than terminal illness, where at least one knows that the misery will end, whereas my life may go on for many, many years."

What can those of us who sympathize with a justified suicide by a handicapped person do to help? As the legal climate now stands in Western society, assistance is particularly dangerous. When we have statutes on the books permitting lawful physician aid-in-dying for the terminally ill, I believe that along with this reform there will come a more tolerant attitude to the other exceptional cases. These are so few that they do not justify special legislation—"hard cases make poor law" as the saying goes.

If handicapped persons and a helper feel they

must proceed with euthanasia, the matter having been carefully considered and there being no alternative, then exceptional care must be taken regarding method, privacy for the act, and subsequent secrecy. There is another saying: "Necessity hath no law." At the very least, the friend must function as a sounding board for the discussion of the pros and cons of the decision, and should carefully consider giving moral support.

My conclusion after fourteen years of watching such cases is that close relatives get greater mercy from the courts than do friends. I suppose it is the old feeling of blood bonds and kinship influencing the judges. Sometimes, however, there is only a friend who is available or will help.

CHAPTER NINE

SELF-STARVATION

Some people feel that starving themselves to death is the ideal euthanasia. There are numerous reports of extremely old people dying this way, and there is no reason to doubt them. But it is not as easy as it sounds. There are many factors to consider.

Medical studies that detail the effects of death by starvation are remarkable in their absence. It does not seem to be a subject with which doctors wish to get involved. There are some studies that report the effects of fasting as acts of protest. Most of these, thankfully, ended in a decision to cease the campaign and live.

These reports tell us that after approximately 20 percent of body weight loss, illness of one sort or another begins to set in, notably severe indigestion, muscle weakness, and—worst of all—mental incapacity. The health of the individual determines which illness comes first. A fit human in his or her forties can fast about forty days before life is seriously threatened. After that, there is a high risk of death. Exactly when this will occur will vary from person to person.

In some cases self-starvation can be very painful. In 1987 after a court in Colorado gave Hector Rodas permission to starve himself to death (he was a quadriplegic), morphine had to be administered to kill the pain of fatal dehydration. In the fifteen days it took Rodas, who had good medical care, to die he constantly slipped in and out of a coma. I believe it would have been more compassionate, once the court had given the green light, to have administered a fatal overdose. But the law did not permit this.

Physicians assure us that the starvation of a patient in a persistent vegetative state causes no suffering, and is humane so long as there is good nursing care, which would include moistening of the lips. A person in a deep coma feels no pain and usually dies in ten to fourteen days. Of course, most such patients have been unconscious for several years and have already deteriorated physically.

A Hemlock member of my acquaintance who was 88, suffering from what I call "terminal old age" after a mild stroke and congestive heart failure, still took thirty-three days to die from self-starvation. Even though she had considered the decision very carefully and was determined to die, that did not speed things up. She also stopped taking all her heart medicines. She took half a cup of water each day and moistened her lips with ice cubes. Three days before her death she began having mild hallucinations, which her doctor treated with Thorazine. After that she slept constantly and died peacefully at her daughter's home.

Her daughter told me, "Needless to say, it was painful to watch her deterioration. I was surprised that she survived so long because I thought that once she made up her mind she would quickly die —partly because we stopped the digoxin but more significantly because she was so strong willed. I finally suggested to her the possibility that her fighting to die might be life-asserting. She then relaxed more and repeated: 'I am at peace.' As the days passed she often stated that she felt very lucky to be experiencing feelings of love and goodwill to all."

Self-starvation has a distinct appeal for some. It is essentially an independent action, taking responsibility for your own death, involving no others, demonstrating strength of desire to die at this point, because of unacceptable quality of life. But the possibility of further illness before death, its effect on loved ones, and the uncertain length of the process, must be carefully considered.

Unless the persons starving themselves to death were in the hands of most conservative, reactionary physicians, there should be no legal trouble. The law does not permit force-feeding. Numerous court cases in America and Britain have repeatedly underlined that no medical treatment can be administered without the patient's consent, even in life-threatening conditions.

CHAPTER TEN

The Will to Die and "Miracle Cures"

An aunt of mine died recently in her eighties from a perforated bowel. She also had numerous other illnesses which, singly or in combination, would eventually have killed her. It was a matter of which illness got her first. She longed to die. "I pray to God to take me now," she would say. But she lingered on for months and suffered physically and mentally. She was so debilitated by her illness that life gave her no pleasure. While she recognized my work in the field of euthanasia, and spoke approvingly of it, her religious beliefs would not permit her to accelerate the end in any way. I respected that.

The will to die is not, in my view, sufficient alone to bring about death. It would be nice if that were all that were necessary. I have heard direct accounts of people who were terribly sick with one or two terminal illnesses who have made planned and determined attempts at suicide, hovered on the brink of death, and failed because of drug interactions that neutralized the lethal effects. In these cases I am convinced that if it were possible to will oneself to death, some would have succeeded because they were so close to the end anyway.

Some people disagree with the foregoing statements. They have confidently told me that all they will need to do when they are terminal is to get into the right frame of mind and within a day or so stop breathing. Some doctors who specialize in care of geriatric patients tell me that there are rare occasions they have heard a very old, sick person announce, "I'm going to die today." And the individual did.

In the 1990 movie *Longtime Companion*, there is an emotional scene where a young gay man suffering from advanced AIDS dies. Film critic David Jansen in his review in *Newsweek* speaks of the dying man's gay lover "helping him to die." The help referred to is better described as "giving permission to die." Over and over, at the sick man's bedside, the lover urges, "Let go. It's all right to let go. Let go." And the sick man dies. Again, we are dealing with fiction, of course, and we are not told in the film precisely how long the dying process took or how close the patient was to death when the "permission" was given.

Beware of taking ideas about death and dying from books and films. The accounts have almost always been abbreviated and sanitized and are sometimes (as mentioned previously) downright wrong.

Having stated my skepticism, however, I do believe that a well-thought-out willingness to die, and also express permission from the loved ones to depart, does help, if only a bit. It frees the patient from familial and social obligations to fight anymore. In certain cases the end might be precipitated by not taking any more medications. Stopping drug therapy to bring about death is risky, however, and may cause suffering. Of course, if a patient is connected to life-support equipment and elects to have it stopped, that settles the matter.

Summing up, it is my view that the will to die in euthanasia cases is preferable and helpful but should not be relied upon as the definitive release mechanism.

On the other side of the coin, a lot of people wonder about the possibility of a so-called "miracle cure" being announced the day after they have deliberately ended their life. It is perfectly natural, when we have a serious disease, to hope that the long-awaited scientific breakthrough is going to happen here and now to save us.

Medical science has made tremendous advances during the past fifty years, and research and technology march forward on many fronts. The fact remains, however, that many types of cancer are not curable, although early detection and sophisticated treatment saves many lives and prolongs others. There is, for instance, currently no cure for Alzheimer's disease, lupus, and amyotrophic lateral sclerosis (Lou Gehrig's disease).

My observation of the trends in modern medicine leads me to believe that the eventual answer to most of these diseases will come from preventive measures against ailments to which we are prone, rather than cure of an illness which has already taken hold. That, of course, remains to be seen.

I cannot find any evidence of overnight miracle cures in medical history. Penicillin, for instance, was discovered in the mid-1930s but did not come onto the market until the second half of the 1940s, and has saved many lives. Enormous progress has been made in combating leukemia in children, but reading the medical literature shows that it was a battle fought over at least a decade. At one stage the drug Interferon was internationally hailed as the answer to most cancers; with further testing, it proved to be of small help.

In the event of a complete cure for a disease being suddenly found, it is unlikely to help a patient who has already been seriously damaged by the ravages of the disease. Vital organs or important tissue may have been destroyed, which is what is bringing the patient to the brink of death and stimulating the desire to have control over that event. Additionally, many drug treatments—notably intense chemotherapy—cause damage to the body while at the same time fighting off the disease. A miracle cure, regardless of how miraculous, would, if it happened, undoubtedly be more effective at the beginning of an illness than in the final stages.

Ask your physician about promising research in the illness for which you are being treated. If there is any, get copies of the medical literature so that you can draw your own conclusions after a further discussion with your physician. Watch the medical sections of the weekly newsmagazines and newspapers—progress in medicine is something upbeat which the media love to report. Take anything you learn back to your physician for a joint evaluation.

Positive progress in medicine comes only after years of dogged research and testing, followed by elaborate evaluation by a government agency—in America, the Food and Drug Administration—with the goal of assuring that no drugs which are approved have harmful side effects.

Pious persons may believe in medical miracles and that is their right. Yet despite all the medical treatment in the world, death will eventually come to us all. It is up to the judgment of each individual to determine when medical treatment should be discontinued or life brought to an end.

CHAPTER ELEVEN

Storing Drugs

Once you have secured your cache of lethal drugs as insurance against an undesirable form of dying, how do you keep them safe and maintain freshness? This is a great worry for many people since they are not expecting to have to use them for some time yet! Remember, life is well worth living to its fullest extent. Here are some tips on preserving the quality of drugs.

Where

Do not open the container at all if you can possibly help it. The original, unopened container is the first line of security. If you have opened it, then remove the cotton or any other packing; if not opened, leave it alone.

Do not put drugs in the freezer unless you are absolutely sure that they are in a sealed, watertight, metal container. Neither the plastic containers in which drugs are usually dispensed by pharmacies, nor plastic film containers, will keep out the frost.

An amber-colored plastic container is preferable to a clear one because it filters out light. A glass container is preferable to a plastic one because glass is chemically inert and cannot affect the contents. (Wine keeps for centuries in bottles.) My cache is Vesperax which I bought in Switzerland. I keep it in its original foil in a glass jar with a tight lid in a closet.

It is best to keep an unopened container in a cupboard or drawer at room temperature. Make sure that no one else, particularly children, can get access to this poison.

Avoid kitchens, bathrooms, and laundry rooms. They are likely to be damp, and vary in temperature, at least some of the time. You should also keep drugs away from lights, sunshine, or heat sources.

Shelf Life

The main factor in shelf life is how fresh the drug is when it is received from the pharmacist. Has it been sitting in a pharmaceutical warehouse for years? Or on the druggist's shelf for a long period?

If a drug a pharmacist has purchased is dated to be used by the end of the month, and it is expected to be used for treatment purposes by about that time, the pharmacist is legally entitled to sell it. *Therefore, when you are buying your intended lethal dose, be particular to ask the expiration date of the drug you are getting.* (Your container almost certainly will not give it but the pharmacist will know.)

As a rule of thumb, drugs carefully stored in the manner I've described in this chapter will keep for five years before any deterioration sets in. The U.S. Food and Drug Administration tends to shorten shelf life periods rather than lengthen them. Thus the unwary customer is protected from inferiority.

Even after five years, most deterioration will be slight. To compensate for this possible shortfall in toxicity, add one extra capsule or tablet to every ten of the recommended lethal dose.

When the CBS television program *60 Minutes* did a segment on Hemlock members in Tucson, Arizona, who were going over the border to Mexico, armed with my other book, *Let Me Die Before I Wake*, and purchasing drugs for storage, they featured a member who kept her "insurance" in a hat box in her closet. That is as good a place as any.

Unfortunately, that program, plus an ABC-TV movie of the week, *When the Time Comes*, both gave an impression that drugs which were only available by prescription in the United States could be easily purchased over the counter in Mexico. It was never that easy, and, worse, the Mexican authorities have subsequently begun to clamp down on drug sales. (See Chapter 18 on how to get the magic pills.)

As in Mexico, Switzerland has seen an increase in the purchase of lethal drugs among those planning euthanasia in the future. This has led to pressure from the government and the source has stopped.

CHAPTER TWELVE

Who Shall Know?

Whom do you want to know about your death, and do you want them also to know that you chose to bring your own life to a close? I have no advice about the first part of the question, of course, but I do recommend that you are frank about the second. Nothing is worse than ill-informed gossip and, once you are gone, there is no chance for you to set the record straight.

It is imperative that your loved ones know what you are contemplating. Do not surprise or shock them. Offhandedly informing them that you are a member of the Hemlock Society [or similar organization outside America] is one opening gambit. If there is no reaction the first time, mention it again later. They may have been surprised and not had time to think about it fully. Do this while you are healthy, if possible. Don't leave it until it's too late.

There may be more support in your family than you realize. One woman I know was keeping it a tight family secret that she was planning to help her mother to die. After the funeral, she discovered that her aunt (her mother's sister) was a charter member of Hemlock. "It would have been so useful to have had Auntie's support," she said. "I just never dreamed she was on that wave-length."

Additionally, tell your closest friends about your intentions. In her final months, my first wife, Jean, would drop it into conversation with her girlfriends when her illness was being discussed: 'I'm not going to the end, you know. I shall do something about it." One of the friends remembered these hints vividly and when I was under investigation in 1978 for assisted suicide she told the police this. I believe it helped me by demonstrating whose intention it was, for although it must have been a close judgment by the prosecutor's office, I was not charged with any offense.

It all depends on your circumstances in life, of course, but an alternative might be to leave a letter to your best friend setting out your reasons for accelerating your demise and saying good-bye at the same time. Ask to have it circulated.

Will it get into the newspapers?

Whether the media wishes to report your death depends very much on who you are. I have read dozens of obituaries of major and minor public figures which say, quite casually, that the person took her life and from what she was suffering. The act of self-destruction is usually not in the head-line nor the first paragraph. I also see death announcements which say that the person belonged to Hemlock and, instead of flowers, requests donations be sent to the society. Public attitude about rational suicide has changed immensely in the past ten years.

The suicide of Janet Adkins in June 1990 was treated as sensational news because Dr. Jack Kevorkian, a pathologist, who helped her to die with his so-called "suicide machine" announced it brazenly in order to try to shock medical opinion. It was then a unique event, and undoubtedly very useful in stirring public opinion about euthanasia. Ms. Adkins was a Hemlock member before her illness.

I asked a reporter on *The Oregonian*, her local newspaper in Portland, if, in the same medical circumstances, she had purchased a gun and gone home and shot herself, would that have been given any space?

"We wouldn't have mentioned it," he replied.

It may seem that there is always reporting of euthanasia cases. The truth is you only hear about the tip of the iceberg, those controversial actions like Kevorkian's or keenly disputed court cases such as Nancy Cruzan's. Take it from me, many hundreds of cases of active and passive euthanasia go undetected, or unreported. And we should all be thankful for that as long as the law is in such a confused state.

CHAPTER THIRTEEN

INSURANCE

A curious feature of my work is that one of the most asked questions over fourteen years has been whether suicide—or self-deliverance or autoeuthanasia, call it what you like—negates life insurance policies. On the other hand, I have only come across one such actual problem. Of course there may be others of which I am not aware.

Gerald Buck was a 51-year-old teacher of industrial arts in Boulder, Colorado, when in July 1986 he was persuaded by an insurance agent to let two long-standing insurance policies lapse and, after a medical examination showed him healthy, to take out a new policy. By October of the same year Mr. Buck became seriously ill with cancer of the esophagus. He had radical surgery followed by chemotherapy but his condition only worsened. Mr. Buck had a tube which drained fluids from his back, was fed through a chest catheter, and suffered a great deal of pain, nausea, and abdominal spasms. Toward the end of February 1987, he left the hospital for a brief home visit. After talking to his wife and parents for a while, he went upstairs and shot himself.

Western States Life Insurance refused to pay

his widow the $25,000 benefit on the policy because his death was by suicide within the one-year time limit specified by Colorado law. Mrs. Buck took the insurance company to court, arguing that the primary cause of her husband's death was cancer. If he had chosen to forgo all treatment, as is not unusual in such a serious case of cancer, he would have died sooner and the family would not have lost the insurance benefit.

The widow's lawyers argued in court that the definition of suicide contemplated by the company did not encompass situations involving the terminally ill person who subsequent to the effective date of the policy chooses to take his or her life rather than face physical and financial deterioration. They contended that the term "suicide" is ambiguous.

The judge agreed with the insurance company's argument that the policy had a suicide exclusion clause with a time limit. The case went to the Colorado Court of Appeals which upheld the decision of the lower court.

The majority of life insurance policies today have a provision that death benefits will not be paid if the insured person commits suicide within a certain period, usually two years, but sometimes one, as in Colorado. In the event of suicide, the company is merely required to return the premiums already paid.

The time limit is set to preclude fraud by persons who want their family to benefit by the taking of their life. There is an assumption that few suicidal people will wait two years before carrying out the act. The insurance company has the burden of proof to establish whether the insured's death was suicide.

My advice is that if you are considering self-deliverance from a terminal illness, look at the dates on your policies. If they are more than two years old, your family is safe. Read the fine print of the policy to see if there are relevant clauses. In general, it is not wise to take out new policies in the late stages of your life. If you do, try to keep the old ones going too. Remember, Mr. Buck's condition must have been developing for years yet still escaped detection at his insurance checkup. Three months later he was terminally ill. Our lives hang by a slender thread.

CHAPTER FOURTEEN

Will There Be an Autopsy?

Many people worry about whether there will be an autopsy after their death. Either they dread the thought of the pathologist's knife after life's end, or the fact that their suicide will be recorded or even published.

Many of us are not bothered about being labeled a suicide at the end. We know that our friends are aware that it was not done out of cowardice or escapism but from long-held rational beliefs. Yet I know from my office correspondence that some people still see both forms of suicide—rational and emotional—as a stigma. They want to know about the chance of autopsies.

An autopsy is a postmortem examination of the corpse by a physician, a trained pathologist, in order to ascertain the actual—instead of estimated—cause of death. It involves dissecting the body to examine and perhaps remove vital organs for testing in another laboratory. Autopsies started in the late eighteenth century. They have provided the foundation of most medical knowledge that we now possess.

Contrary to wide belief, autopsies are not compulsory, except in hospitals in Bulgaria, Hungary,

Italy, and Poland. Since three of these countries are no longer under the Soviet sphere of influence, that may change. In Norway, Iceland, and France they are mandatory, too, but the family of the deceased may object. The rest of the Western world says that consent of the family is always required—except where law enforcement authorities have reason to suspect that a crime or an unnatural death may have occurred.

This requirement of consent to an autopsy in English-speaking countries comes from English common law which gives families limited rights to the body after death. Even written instructions left by the deceased can be overridden by the family. This has been modified somewhat in the past twenty years by various laws which allow for advance documentation of a desire to donate body parts to medical science. However, without specific organ harvesting arrangements or the suspicion of a crime, the old law remains: doctors must have permission from family before carrying out an autopsy.

Until the 1950s, half the people who died in American hospitals were autopsied. Today that figure has fallen to under 13 percent. The rate remains higher in teaching hospitals, for obvious reasons, but is down as low as 5 percent in community hospitals and 1 percent in nursing homes.

The reasons for the drop are numerous and varied: medical science has given doctors remarkable diagnostic tools that ought to pinpoint a correct malady (although some studies have shown an error rate of up to a third); the cost has gone up to about $1,800 per postmortem and insurance companies will not pay; doctors fear being found out in a misdiagnosis and sued by the next of kin.

There are possible benefits from an autopsy. Sometimes what seemed to be a death from a heart attack may have been caused by an accident and be worthy of an insurance claim; if the cause of death is a source of worry for the family, then it may resolve uncertainty and reduce grief; if there is a genetic disorder in the family, the autopsy might spot this and suggest greater care might be taken by the survivors; and autopsies can find and fight previously undetected diseases, especially new ones caused by environmental factors.

Having explained briefly the background to autopsies, we are really concerned here with self-deliverance and the assisted suicide of a dying person. If the police have a slight suspicion of a suicide, they can legally order an autopsy. It is their task to be sure that an assisted suicide is not really cold-blooded murder. My experience indicates that if the investigators are factually aware of serious terminal illness, they will not do so if there is a suicide note that corroborates it. "Why bother?" they reason. I have heard of cases where a sample of the drug used is taken from the intestines for analysis, yet there has been no full autopsy. Detectives just want to know what substance was used. If it was a familiar medication such as a barbiturate from sleeping pills, they are generally satisfied. But an exotic drug like curare would excite their attention.

If asked for permission to perform an autopsy, refuse it. That is a right. If a doctor or law officer asks for a reason for refusing, cite religion (if that is so) or personal ethics. Some religions, notably Orthodox Judaism and Buddhism, forbid any mutilation of a dead body. Moreover, death might pass as "natural causes" if the doctor speedily tells the police just how serious the illness was. So it's wise to have your doctor called in immediately after death.

Your family may not need to call the police, anyway. If a patient has been seen recently by a doctor who is willing to sign the death certificate stating that death was from such-and-such an illness, then the police will not be informed. The period that must elapse between the last doctor visit and death varies from state to state (fourteen days is common), sometimes from county to county. When making your final preparations, telephone the Medical Examiner's Office in your locality. In my telephone book it is in the front pages under the county name, then listed under "Health and Human Services" as "Medical Examiner."

Ask the circumstances under which the examiner must be contacted and what the rule is about how much time must elapse between the last visit to a sick patient and death to enable a physician to automatically sign a death certificate. Ask, too, if the medical examiner keeps a list of people known to be terminally ill and close to the end. That is the case in some parts of Florida, where, because of the high death rate among the unusual amount of elderly, the examiner likes to be fore-warned. If there is such a listing, ask your doctor if the dying patient is on this list.

CHAPTER FIFTEEN

A Private Affair?

To avoid suffering, some people wish to bring their lives to a planned closure without the rest of the world knowing that it was an accelerated end. This may spring from an intense desire for privacy at this most significant point in their life; it may be that the traditional taboo on suicide lingers strongly; or they may wish to avoid offending a loved one who does not sympathize with such actions.

Whatever the motivation, we have to respect their determination and try to come to terms with it. I am frequently approached by people who ask how they can kill themselves but make it appear to be a natural death. My first response is to gently argue that secrecy should not be necessary in these enlightened times. Second, that today there is a widespread understanding and tolerance of rational suicide associated with terminal illness or physically degenerating old age. Sometimes my view prevails in the discussion; often it does not.

Can a person keep self-deliverance a secret? The answer is: not for certain. (It is more likely to be accomplished by happenstance.) True, some lethal drugs are extremely difficult to trace in the body after death, but there is no drug which cannot be found if the pathologist and laboratory colleagues know what they are looking for, or run tests for all the possibilities. I do not propose to name the drugs which are hard to trace because that information could possibly aid people with evil intent toward the lives of others.

There is a further category of people with whose desire for secrecy I am sympathetic—the assister or assisters in the rational suicide of a terminally ill person. They, of course, are at risk of prosecution.

In such cases, advance planning of tactics and statements is essential. It is important to survey the circumstances of the situation—primarily, the desires of the dying person, the nature of the suffering, the nearness of death, and the quality of the relationship. If secrecy is to be attempted, the dying person should write the indemnifying notes described elsewhere in this book and store them in a safe place.

These notes may need to be shown later if questions are asked. In due course, such letters may be destroyed.

In the two cases in which I assisted, silence was my main protection. My approach was to wait and see what transpired. When Jean took an overdose and died, I asked my daughter-in-law to call our family doctor to come and certify death. When his car entered our driveway, I walked out to the orchard and spent time examining the fruit trees.

I was within call if wanted. Apparently he merely checked for signs of life, found none, and immediately signed a death certificate describing the cause as "carcinomatosis." When he drove away I returned to the house.

Three years later when I deliberately chose to make the matter public in order to stir public opinion, I sent the doctor an advance copy of my book *Jean's Way*, so that he would not be surprised when the story emerged. He wrote back that he had never realized that Jean had brought about her own end, although, knowing her character, he was not surprised.

An astonishing coincidence helped the inquiry into my father-in-law's death that I had assisted. When the local police chief came to the house I overheard the doctor explain to him that the dead man was 92 years old, extremely ill, and had taken an overdose. The doctor added that he had been forewarned that this might happen. The police chief's reply was a pleasant surprise to me. "There was a television program about this sort of thing earlier this evening," he remarked. "It seems to be happening a lot."

In fact, the program he chanced to see was a repeat of the *60 Minutes* segment featuring Hemlock members in Tucson, Arizona, going over the border into Mexico in search of lethal drugs to be stored for possible later use. The program showed the travelers holding out my book, *Let Me Die Before I Wake*, for the store assistants to more easily understand the names of certain drugs. Neither the doctor nor the police chief asked who I was, and, of course, I did not volunteer the information! That was the end of the matter so far as the authorities were concerned.

Television programs like the one shown that evening help induce a climate of understanding that protects a person who feels that a moral obligation to assist the sufferer transcends the current law.

To summarize: If you want the euthanasia of your loved one to be private, think things through extremely carefully. At all times, before and after, act and speak with great reserve and caution. Above all, do not implicate yourself through written or oral explanations which are better not offered. Say nothing. Maintain the courage of your convictions. Let others find out only if they wish to.

CHAPTER SIXTEEN

Support Groups for the Dying

Some people want their passage from life to death to be extremely private, the experience shared only with those closest to them. Others want to be able to talk about it with others who have some knowledge of the subject. As the taboo on voluntary euthanasia has fallen away in America in recent years, and as the Hemlock Society has gained wider acceptability, an important development has been the growth of support groups or networks where people can meet and talk within Hemlock's nearly one hundred chapters.

Usually one of the chapter's leaders who has experience in psychological counseling initiates and leads the group. A typical group comprises a few people who have helped a loved one to die, some who are facing this role, and a few who are dying and considering self-deliverance. Occasionally hospice volunteers who are also Hemlock supporters join the little group.

There is, of course, no agenda at such meetings. A few people tend to start by sharing their sorrow at the recent loss of family or friend. It moves on to talking of feelings about confronting one's own death. Often there is talk about the problems of coping with the health care system and its expense, as well as exploring alternatives to traditional medicine. Ways to keep up one's spirits when terminally ill are frequently discussed.

As one member put it to me: "It makes me feel good to be able to talk with people who are also really focused, and not afraid to talk openly about death and dying." Even in the face of impending death, members of such groups often feel relief and delight at taking back some control over their own lives.

Only Hemlock members may attend these support groups—which are completely separate from the chapter's regular public meetings—and then only by first contacting the coordinator. People who are suicidal, depressive, or suffering from other kinds of severe emotional disturbance are not appropriate for such groups and are referred elsewhere for help. Outside speakers are not used; this type of meeting involves purely kindred spirits talking together about their common problems.

Discussion of how to end one's own life is also not permitted, since this could possibly infringe the law. When this issue comes up, as it inevitably does, those attending are referred to Hemlock's printed literature. But the tough realities of dealing with dying are not shirked and are dealt with as best as possible at the meeting, if only by exchanging experiences.

If you or someone you love is facing death, and if it is causing you great anguish, it may be advisable to seek help from a therapist if no support group such as I have just mentioned is available. A therapist who defines himself or herself as a "family therapist" is most likely to be able to counsel on problems of dying.

Be cautious about telling any health professional that your terminal illness is causing you to think about suicide. Feel your way toward that particular admission extremely slowly, if at all. The law in many places requires health professionals to take action to prevent possible suicides, and I have heard of a few cases where dying people who talked of future self-deliverance ended up being forcibly committed for two or three days in the psychiatric ward of a hospital. It was a devastating experience.

Most health professionals today are sensitive to carefully expressed feelings on euthanasia, but there is the occasional physician, nurse, or mental health worker who rigidly applies the letter of the law on attempted suicide. If you are hurting, seek counseling but do not be too frank to start with.

CHAPTER SEVENTEEN

LETTERS TO BE WRITTEN

Upon your death, one or more letters should be beside your body when it is found. You may also want to mail letters to personal friends telling them what you are doing and why, but that is a very individual choice.

The most important letter is what has historically been called "the suicide note." It must clearly state why you are taking your life, that you accept sole responsibility, and that nobody else persuaded you. In the event that you are discovered before death has taken place, you must demand that you are not to be disturbed but allowed to die. Using the law of informed consent, you cannot be touched or treated without your permission. If you were revived you could, technically, sue for battery.

Attach to the letter copies of your Living Will and Durable Power of Attorney for Health Care. This is evidence of advance planning and helps to eradicate any suspicion of hasty, ill-considered dying. Refer to these documents in your final note.

Your last letter, preferably not typewritten but in your own handwriting, and signed, could be cast broadly in these following terms:

I have decided to end my life because the suffering from . . . disease is unbearable to me. I consider I have lived a full and useful life but I no longer wish it to continue.

This decision is known to others but the final decision has been mine alone in a normal state of mind. I am a member of the Hemlock Society [or similar organization if in another country] and agree with its credo. I have made the choice to die now. No one helped me.

My Living Will and Durable Power of Attorney for Health Care are attached as evidence of my carefully considered wishes with regard to my death.

If I am discovered before I have stopped breathing, I forbid anyone, including doctors or paramedics, to attempt to revive me. If I am revived, I shall sue anyone who aided in this.

Signed ....   *Dated* ....

Make two copies of this note because the police or coroner, if they become involved, will take the top copy and your survivors or attorney will need a copy also.

If you are unfortunately obliged to end your life in a hospital or motel, it is gracious to leave a note apologizing for the shock and inconvenience to the staff. I have also heard of an individual leaving a generous tip to a motel staff.

You should consider leaving letters to loved ones saying why you are taking your own life. Explain that you did not wish to tell them exactly when, to protect them from legal involvement. Experience has taught me that those left behind can be hurt by not being personally involved, even if only on a remote basis. A gentle, loving note of explanation could avoid a good deal of anguish among those you least wish to hurt.

If you feel unable to leave a long letter explaining why you are accelerating your end, use a tape recorder. Mark the cassette clearly "My Final Statement."

You should also have made a Last Will and Testament, using an attorney, to dispose of your worldly goods and wealth, however large or small. Since those you leave behind will be suffering the emotional trauma of your death, they will thank you for leaving your financial affairs in order, alleviating more stress. It is astonishing how many people do not make a will. Legal scholars say about 85 percent of the population dies intestate.

CHAPTER EIGHTEEN

How Do You Get the Magic Pills?

For the past ten years of its existence, the most persistently difficult question put to me at Hemlock has been: "Your book *Let Me Die Before I Wake* is an excellent guide to self-deliverance from terminal illness, but where do you get the pills?"

Therefore, I have recently been reviewing the options on the lawful purchase of lethal drugs suitable for voluntary euthanasia. I can confidently report that in the last decade physicians' attitudes have changed; a good many, particularly if they are under 45, will discreetly prescribe lethal drugs in appropriate cases. (More on this later.)

As noted above, it has become more difficult to purchase suitable drugs in Mexico and Switzerland without prescription. Perhaps Hemlock is the victim of its own members' news service; authorities over the border have become nervous.

Travelers report that Spain, Brazil, Singapore, and Hong Kong are the easiest places to secure drugs, but how often does the average person get to such exotic spots?

Experts say that roughly half of the barbiturates

made in the United States—the drug of choice in self-deliverance—find their way onto the black market. But the average Hemlock member is not the sort of person who wants to hunt dark inner-city streets in order to purchase "Reds" (the street name for Seconal) illicitly. There is always the risk that some substances bought in the street are below strength or contaminated.

Of course, it is always worth an inspection of your medicine cabinet for any barbiturates left over from previous illnesses suffered by you or your family. If the drugs have been kept in their original container—although briefly opened in the past—and sitting in a drug cabinet, they are unlikely to have deteriorated very much.

To be safe, it is a good rule to add one pill for every ten to the intended lethal dosage, if the drugs are more than five years old. This should compensate for any possible deterioration in toxicity.

But, as we have been pointing out in *Hemlock Quarterly* for some time, surveys indicate that the medical profession remains our best ally in self-deliverance. More of our members are reporting in the last few years that doctors have helped them to obtain drugs than ever before. This is encouraging.

For example, one physician in general surgery recently wrote to Hemlock on his group practice notepaper: "I have never had a problem in prescribing large amounts of sleeping pills or other medications for patients or their families on request in certain situations. I recognize that people may desire an escape hatch and I feel it is my duty to help provide it.

'I do not look upon them as cheating or lying when they ask me for a prescription in this situation. I feel a patient has a right as an individual to take an overdose in a situation of that kind. I regret that the insurance companies and society at large do not recognize this.'

So what are the best tactics in approaching doctors? Here are my recent conclusions, which have varied only in slight emphasis from page 67 of *Let Me Die Before I Wake*. (Small-print editions up to 1990.)

If Terminal Illness Is Confirmed

Ask your doctor straight out to give you a prescription, citing your condition and your beliefs in the Hemlock philosophy (that a dying adult who is suffering should be entitled to request assisted suicide).

Do not accept vague answers like, "Don't worry! I won't let you suffer." Say that you don't want to take chances, and don't wish to get the doctor into trouble. Coolly suggest two separate prescriptions on different dates each for twenty Seconal (forty being the lethal dose) as a form of protection for the doctor.

Do not be worried about what the doctor thinks about your plan to have self-deliverance as an option if the suffering becomes unbearable. It is not a crime to consider suicide, nor to carry it out. Informing even the most reluctant doctor is good strategy for the future. If called upon by the coroner, the doctor knows of your intention and will report this.

If you are refused help—probably because of personal ethics or fear of the law (unwarranted since no doctor in the United States has ever been convicted of assisted suicide)—then you will have to move on to the next doctor.

Regretably, there is no point in asking Hemlock for the name of sympathetic doctors, because those who help do it only for patients whom they know and trust. With the exception of Dr. Kevorkian, we never hear of physicians who help strangers to die. One physician told me: "The person making a head-on approach may be pleasantly surprised. I myself will provide prescriptions as long as the person is my patient, or someone very close to me."

If you are healthy now but wish to hoard against sudden illness, the direct approach is not advised. Very, very few physicians will prescribe a lethal dose for a fit person. The stigma of being associated with a possible emotional suicide (as distinct from a rational suicide) is too risky.

Here, doctors close to Hemlock advise the indirect, slow approach. Tell your doctor you cannot sleep, and do not demur when Dalmane or Halcion is prescribed.

Return to the doctor's office a few weeks later and complain that these drugs just do not help you sleep. Could you please have something stronger? Chances are that the doctor will then prescribe something like Miltown or Equanil, which are satisfactory for many types of insomnia but completely unsuitable for self-deliverance. Accept these drugs in apparent good faith. You don't have to fill the prescription.

Pay a third visit to the doctor later and firmly complain that your sleep pattern is not helped at all by the prescriptions so far. If the doctor hesitates, hint that you have heard that something like Seconal or Nembutal would probably do the trick, and that you would be very careful with it.

It is a doctor's job to help with your medical problems, and there is now no tool left except barbiturates. Make use of the prescription immediately and hoard at least forty (sixty is best) in a cool, dry place. Be sure it is secure from deliberate or accidental discovery by others.

"Basically, you are duping the doctor," said one physician. "But let's face it, he may not mind being duped. At least he's not involved criminally because there was no intent on his part."

Workers in the worldwide euthanasia movement have noticed two things about physician involvement in assisted suicide for the dying:

1. Physicians will often write out prescriptions for lethal doses if the patient asks by name for a specific drug in a sizable amount. It is part of the code in which the doctor is thinking: I know you might use this for suicide but don't tell me.

2. Some physicians will cooperate and even be on call, if it is known that the patient is dying and

possesses his or her own drugs. "Then the doctor will keep an eye on the patient, see to it that death is coming along," one person involved in many assisted deaths told me.

CHAPTER NINETEEN

Self-Deliverance via the Plastic Bag

When I first started writing about self-deliverance for the terminally ill fourteen years ago, any suggestion of using a plastic bag as well as lethal drugs was repugnant to me.

It seemed undignified as a means of final exit, unaesthetic to those who might view the body; unnecessary because there are some very lethal drugs on the market (physician's prescription only, I'm afraid); and, most crucial of all, frightening because it seemed to involve suffocation.

In my 1981 book, *Let Me Die Before I Wake*, I briefly referred to some people using plastic bags to ensure they were released from their terminal suffering. In the 1986 update, when new chapters were added, including my description of how I would end my own life if I needed release from pain and indignity, I said I would probably use a plastic bag as well as sleeping pills.

I wrote: "There is a 10 percent chance that my body might for some freakish reason ride out the assault of the drugs, or I might vomit despite the precautions.

So I would have on hand a plastic bag. . . ."

I want to underline that conviction: *If you don't*

have the help of a physician to aid the dying, then a plastic bag as well as drugs is highly advisable.

Hemlock has been and always will be in favor of lawful physician aid-in-dying. When reform comes it will make books like this, and *Let Me Die Before I Wake*, redundant, a footnote in social history.

But there are those who are dying now, who are suffering more than they can bear, and who reason that release from life is desirable.

As Hemlock's executive director I more often hear heartening stories of doctors who do provide the drugs for euthanasia, thoughtfully and discreetly. But not all doctors will. Perhaps the relationship with the patient is too erratic; or the doctor has different ethical views. Some doctors are ignorant of euthanasia techniques. Anyway, a surprising number of people, particularly devoted couples, want to handle the process themselves. It is their final act of love together.

Most people take great trouble to have the correct drugs and prepare for their exit with care and devotion. Nothing is too much trouble. Often *Let Me Die Before I Wake* is read and reread, passages are marked, particularly in the final chapters.

In the vast majority of cases, the drugs work and in any time between twenty minutes and one hour the person is dead. Sometimes it is longer, say, two hours, but that is exceptional.

Occasionally—and this is the purpose of this book—I hear the odd case of a terminal person who took what was obviously a lethal dose of drugs in the recommended manner, and either did not die or lingered on for one or two days. It is rare, but it does happen. And it causes great distress to the survivors who, in the best interest of the loved one, have been supportive.

From my discussions with families and doctors, it seems that these occasional cases of failure are related to drugs interacting or, more likely, tolerance. In an ideal self-deliverance, the patient avoids all drugs for several days beforehand. But that is not always possible, especially where severe pain is involved.

Thus I want to emphasize the necessity of the plastic bag in self-deliverance.

I also want to amend slightly, in the light of experience and discussions with physicians within the euthanasia movement, what I wrote in the early editions of *Let Me Die Before I Wake.*

It is preferable that the plastic bag not fit tightly over the head, but be moderately loose. It is very important that it be firmly tied around the neck with either a large rubber band or a ribbon. No more air must come in. Some people use pantyhose.

One member recently asked me how she could inflate the bag! I told her that it's deflation that's needed!

With the plastic bag secured around the neck, the dying person uses up oxygen in the air, replacing it with carbon dioxide, and leaving behind nitrogen that permits breathing. A human cannot live on carbon dioxide and nitrogen alone.

Dr. Colin Brewer (MB, MRCS, MRCPsych) has

written: "You can commit suicide just with a plastic bag but it gets a little uncomfortable because you breathe out carbon dioxide and, as the carbon dioxide increases, then the body adjusts to this and you find yourself breathing more deeply and that can be mildly distressing, though it is not the same as having your respiration actually blocked."

That is why I do not recommend the plastic bag alone (as prisoners who are suicidal are sometimes obliged to do). It is thus necessary to have taken a fair amount of sleeping pills to eliminate that slight discomfort. Sufficient sleeping pills to ensure two hours' sleep should be enough.

So, the plastic bag should be loose, but not huge since that will take longer. The pills should be fast-acting sleep inducers. You can find this out by testing a couple on yourself previously. Each reaction is different.

Should you use a clear plastic bag or an opaque one? That's a matter of taste. Loving the world as I do, I'll opt for a clear one if I have to.

Because exhaled air is always at body temperature (approximately 98.6°F or 37°C) and 100 percent relative humidity, the use of a plastic bag may create an unpleasant hot and humid, muggy, stuffy feeling. Many would find this a "suffocating" sensation long before the oxygen falls to a level that would induce or enhance a lack of awareness of this discomfort.

This distress might create a panic in which the person removes the bag, despite his or her resolve. Success might be enhanced by the use of an old-fashioned ice bag or cold compress applied to the forehead or neck, or just by the expectation and awareness of this effect so as to avoid an unpleasant surprise.

A device some people have used to stop the plastic bag being in contact with their nostrils and mouth is to wear a paper filter mask used when painting or sanding. This can be bought at a hardware store quite cheaply. The little mask obviates the fear of the plastic being sucked in.

When using the plastic bag technique, it is best done from a sitting position, holding the bag open at the neck until falling asleep. As the person falls asleep, the grip on the elastic bands relaxes and the bag closes, cutting off oxygen.

Why not have a trial run? So long as you are fit and alert, you can take the bag off easily. A colleague of mine in Hemlock, Don Shaw, of Chicago, claims that an experiment is helpful. He told me:

"I decided that I should find out for myself how it feels to put the plastic bag over my head and use the rubber bands. I was amazed at how unfrightening it was, but I did learn something important about the rubber bands. Namely, that first one should open the bag all the way and see for yourself how much air it can hold, etc. First I tried to get the rubber bands on after I put the bag over my head and it was almost impossible. Then, after opening the bag again, I put the rubber bands on and put the bag on like a hat and it worked easily.

I also was able to find out that two average rubber bands were adequate.

"I was so impressed with the experiment that I performed it for our Hemlock chapter meeting a week or so later. Everyone was both amused and impressed. I urged them to go home and try it on for themselves in order to get more comfortable with the whole concept."

There is one other way, of course, if you have a willing accomplice, but it has a technical legal risk. Some people make a pact with a friend that the plastic bag will be put on after, say, two hours if the drugs for some reason have not ended life.

Remember that assistance in suicide, no matter how compassionate and how sincerely requested, remains a crime for now. True, it is rarely prosecuted, mainly because the authorities never hear about it. It is the secret crime of our times.

The actual helping of the person constitutes the crime by demonstrating intent. Intent is necessary for successful prosecution. So it is preferable if the person wanting deliverance does it alone. There is no legal risk in removing the bag once the person stops breathing. Removal also reduces the chance of police or medical examiners suspecting suicide.

CHAPTER TWENTY

Going Together?

Two friends of mine in their late seventies were in an aircraft when it had engine trouble. The captain warned the passengers to prepare for an emergency landing. "I was very scared," said the man. I asked his wife how she felt. "I felt a certain sense of relief that we were going to die together," she replied.

Such feelings are by no means uncommon among couples married a long time or who have built an interdependent relationship. The fear of being the one left behind is constantly on their minds. The prospect of loneliness, financial shortage, and the possibility of going through their own terminal illness without the comfort of a supportive mate is forbidding.

Cynthia Koestler took her life rather than be without her husband, the writer Arthur Koestler (*Darkness at Noon*, etc.). He was dying at the age of 77 but she was perfectly healthy and 55. In 1983 they were found dead in their living room, seated in separate chairs. Beside them was a glass of whiskey, two empty wineglasses containing a residue of white powder, and an empty bottle of Tuinal (a brand of secobarbital no longer marketed). Arthur had already published his eloquent suicide note, and Cynthia, whose death surprised her friends, left a note which said in part: "I cannot live without Arthur, despite certain inner resources."

The world of religion and philosophy in America was shocked in 1975 when Henry and Elizabeth Van Dusen took their lives. Dr. Van Dusen was one of the most important theologians in the Protestant church. Both were elderly and in extremely poor health. In her last note, Mrs. Van Dusen said in part: "There are too many helpless old people who without modern medical care would have died, and we feel God would have allowed them to die when their time had come."

Some couples choose to die together, regardless of whether both are in poor health, or only one. It is more likely to happen when both are ailing. Such double exits should be neither promoted nor condemned. Who are we to look in the minds of others? That the couple would wish to die together is a tribute to the strength of a loving relationship.

The eminent philosopher Joseph Fletcher says: "We should look at every case on its merits and refuse to be bound indiscriminately by universal rules of right and wrong, whether they claim to rest on religious or pragmatic grounds."

With younger people, when it is known that one partner is dying, it is not uncommon for the healthy spouse to declare immediately that they will die at the same time. Usually there is later a change of mind. The dying person often persuades the partner not to make things worse for the family by dying as well, and a sense of responsibility takes over.

I have known people who swear they will die with their spouse, but who alter their thinking, and a year or two later I hear that they have married again. People have inner resources that allow them to go on living despite horrendous tragedies.

One couple of my acquaintance found the wife, in her forties, with inoperable cancer. She decided on self-deliverance but was horrified to find that her husband was insistent that he would die simultaneously. This cameo illustrates how they approached death in very different ways: one day she was seen dancing lightly around the lawn, gently flapping her arms and humming merrily. "What are you doing?" asked her husband. "I'm practicing to be an angel," she responded. Her husband ran indoors in tears. It seems that by actions such as these that she eventually convinced her husband to view death differently. After a farewell champagne and caviar party, she took her life with his assistance. Three years later he remarried.

For a devoted couple at the end of their lives, who are in physically degenerating conditions, a clearly thought-out, mutually agreed and justifiable double suicide is an option we should respect. If we are asked and it is appropriate, we may even assist.

With younger couples, it is obviously an option of very last resort. In all my experience I have not come across a case where it was carried out.

CHAPTER TWENTY-ONE

WHEN IS THE TIME TO DIE?

"The strangest whim has seized me. After all, I think I will not hang myself today," wrote G.K. Chesterton, facetiously, in *A Ballade of Suicide.* In real life, the timing of when to end one's life when terminally ill is the most overwhelmingly difficult decision. Nobody wants to die, yet life with an incurable or degenerative illness can be unacceptable for some people. Therefore, death is the preferred alternative.

Sometimes people call me and want to talk about when they shall die. I am extremely careful not to offer an opinion, but let myself merely be a sounding board, a sympathetic ear.

Usually what I hear comes down to two issues. The first is that the person is not at all sure that death is close, but they *think* it may be. I suggest they have further talks with the physician about the progress of their illness, and ask if there are any other therapies which might be tried. That talk might clear the air.

When my first wife, Jean, was close to the end, with the cancer spread into many parts of her body, she asked me one morning: "Is this the day?" Some people have interpreted that question as implying that I was in control of the timing. Not so. The pact which Jean and I had made included *sharing* the decision.

Nine months earlier she had said: "The one thing that worries me is that I won't be in any position to make the right decision, what with my being knocked senseless with all these drugs. I might be too daft to know whether I'm doing the right thing or not, but I shall have a good idea when I've had enough of the pain. So I want you to promise me that when I ask you if this is the right time to kill myself, you will give me an honest answer one way or another and we must understand, both you and I, that I'll do it right at that very moment. You won't question my right and you will give me the means to do it."

I was Jean's safety device against a too-early self-deliverance. While I did not want her to die, I was willing to take my share of the responsibility of decision-making if it brought her peace. Assisting in difficult decisions is an essential responsibility of a loving relationship.

Secondly, there is often an underlying and healthy reason why people who are terminal are not taking steps to die at a certain point. Something is happening on the fringe of their lives and they want to be part of it: a wedding, a birth, an examination result, or similar life-affirming event.

The bottom line is that they really are not ready to die if they are questioning the advisability of it. My advice to people in this quandary is: if you are in any doubt, then do not do it. Make the most of the time you have left.

"I prefer old age to the alternative," remarked Maurice Chevalier, the French entertainer, who died in 1972 at the age of 84.

Incompetency

By far the most difficult problem concerns victims of Alzheimer's disease. This illness affects the brain as it insidiously destroys a person's ability to think and remember. "I think I'm losing my mind" is a throw-away remark we all make at some time as an excuse for forgetfulness, but we also know as we say it that it has dreaded undertones.

Janet Adkins challenged us all on this issue when she took her life with Dr. Kevorkian's help in 1990. (See Chapter Two in Part Two for full description.) She waited only a year until the first symptoms of Alzheimer's began to show. The bulk of health professionals quoted in the media condemned her timing, arguing that she had a good deal of quality life still left. Undoubtedly she did, but that assertion begs the question of what happens after that point in Alzheimer's when the intellectual deterioration is so serious that the patient becomes incompetent. At that point the patient has lost control, and will be a very sick person for up to ten or fifteen years. It is too late for voluntary euthanasia!

The decision of Mrs. Adkins to die at the time she did probably surprised me less than anybody, because I hear of this happening a great deal in unreported cases. Most of these exits are as a result of degenerative old age. Most times the person has lost a spouse and faces the final months or years alone. There is probably illness, with the prospect of a sudden stroke or debilitating heart attack, which will mean a nursing home for the final years. Most have seen their parents through a grim deathwatch and do not wish to repeat it for their offspring. Such people look back on their lives, count their blessings, and end their existence.

Such actions are hard for us healthy, younger people to understand. I have had to deal with the guilt and anger of relatives and friends, who cry out, "We loved her! We would have done anything! Why did she have to do it now?"

My questioning in response usually elicits that the upset person knew perfectly well that the deceased sincerely believed in voluntary euthanasia. I ask if they had respected the intelligence and character of the deceased up to the time of suicide. Once it sinks in that this was the rational decision of a person whom they admired, acceptance of their death, and the manner of it, begins to grow.

I am not for one moment advocating that elderly people, or patients with degenerative diseases, should take their lives. It is too personal a decision. I am speaking up for tolerance, compassion, and understanding of that most important of civil liberties: the option to govern our own lives, which includes the right to choose to die.

Alternatives

If I should contract Alzheimer's or another mind-altering disease, and become incompetent, I want somebody to whom I have given prior authority to arrange to have my life ended by a doctor when it has reached the point where I am not the human being I am now. Put another way: I wish to be killed when I am a so-called vegetable. ("Vegetable" is not a gracious term when applied to a human being, but it has gained a certain earthy popularity among nonmedical people and certainly expresses their horror of such situations.)

With the complete *Death with Dignity Act*, when it becomes law everywhere, there would be a way of handling the dilemma of those with degenerative diseases, or what I call "terminal old age" in a caring and lawful way.

The proposed law would allow people who had made a positive decision that they did not, at some future date, wish to linger in a nursing home as a result of a stroke or Alzheimer's to sign an advance declaration that they have appointed such-and-such a person to ask their doctor to end their life.

This "instrument" is the Durable Power of Attorney for Health Care as grafted into *The Death with Dignity Act.* To protect against abuse, it would operate with more checks and balances for incompetent patients than with rational patients (who could just sign a request which secured the agree-

ment of two doctors that help with death was justifiable).

For the incompetent patient, there would have
to be additional safeguards. The request by the
surrogate decision-maker for the Durable Power
of Attorney to be implemented at this point would
have to be reviewed by a hospital committee of at
least three persons. The committee would have to
be satisfied that the directive had been properly
executed and witnessed when the patient was
competent, that it had not been revoked, that two
physicians had certified that the patient was terminal in the long term and, finally, that the time
and manner of death had been properly decided
by the surrogate and the treating physician.

At the time of writing there is a trend in the
euthanasia movement to legislate only for physician aid-in-dying for the terminal patient who is
rational. The supporters for this trend argue that
this is more easily understood, is less controversial, and will bring faster results in law reform.

But I believe that to duck responsibility for the
incompetent patient is a serious gap in our humanitarian cause. Take these examples: it was relatively easy for me, philosophically, to help Jean
to die because she was making a competent decision. She was in charge of her death. But Roswell
Gilbert, in Florida in 1985, was faced with an incompetent wife begging to die. (She had
Alzheimer's and osteoporosis.) He felt obliged—
with forty-five years of marriage as his justification
—to act on her behalf. He shot Emily and re-

ceived twenty-five years' imprisonment, commuted in 1990 to five years.

The empathy which most of the public displayed for the "my time is now" decision of Janet Adkins is one illustration of the deep concern many people have about the fate of the incompetent patient. We must offer these victims a better alternative which will enable them to live longer with their disability and also to die with certainty and dignity when the time is right.

CHAPTER TWENTY-TWO

The Final Act

How do you end your own life with certainty and grace?

I believe that everything written in this book is important, but the very core is this chapter, especially if you are unable to have a physician end your life for you. If you are lucky enough to have that help, then Part Two of this book is for the physician's guidance.

Planning and great care are required for self-deliverance with certainty. No terminally ill person sincerely wanting to exit wishes to end up labeled as one of those "crying for help" victims. I do hear occasionally of people botching it and, in those cases where I am able to get at the facts, a slip-up is usually traceable.

The biggest danger is falling asleep before taking sufficient drugs. Years ago a woman complained to me that her husband had swallowed fifty Seconal and drank a bottle of whiskey, but had taken four days to die. I had no answer. A few months later, she called again to say that during spring cleaning she had removed the cushions from the chair in which he had sat, and found about twenty-five Seconal. She admitted that she had not wanted to sit with him while he took the drugs. Therefore she did not see him fall asleep and drop the pills into the chair cushions.

Occasionally drugs will cancel out each other. It is extremely hard to discover all possibilities without the most detailed forensic analysis of each case. A person's metabolism can be a crucial factor. If at all possible, taking of other drugs should be stopped well before the self-deliverance is attempted.

I have helped three people to die—my first wife, my brother, and my father-in-law. My brother was severely brain damaged in an accident, and with entire family agreement, I asked the doctors to disconnect him from life-support equipment. He died four hours later. Both Jean and my father-in-law were very sick people and anxious to die. Jean died in 1975 within fifty minutes by taking a combination of Seconal and codeine. My father-in-law died in 1986 within twenty minutes by ingesting Vesperax (secobarbital and brallobarbital).

The difference of time between the two deaths —fifty minutes as against twenty—I ascribe to my much greater knowledge of practical euthanasia eleven years later. With Jean, I had no knowledge of the importance of the contents of the stomach. Nor did I know anything about taking precautions against nausea, with the result that she vomited some of the drugs, much to my consternation. From these two experiences, and all I have heard over the fourteen years of my involvement in the worldwide euthanasia movement, these are my recommendations.

First of all, some *don'ts*. Do not consider non-prescription drugs, poisons from plants or bushes, nor cleaning fluids like lye. If they do happen to kill you, it will be a painful and lengthy death caused by burning out the lining of your stomach. Shooting and hanging are ugly and extremely traumatic for your loved ones, who, by the violent nature of these methods of self-destruction, cannot be present. They might wish to be with you at the last farewell. Don't use a car exhaust because of the failure risk.

If you have secured the cooperation of a physician, when you are preparing to die, check very carefully that he or she is in town. I have heard of cases where the sympathetic physician was absent and the stand-in threatened to call the authorities.

The two best methods of self-deliverance from a terminal illness—lacking the direct help of a doctor—are from the use of selected prescription drugs, aided by a plastic bag. There are two possible situations:

(a) you have barbiturate drugs such as secobarbital (Seconal) and pentobarbital (Nembutal); or

(b) you have nonbarbiturate drugs such as diazepam (Valium) and propoxyphene (Darvon), or you do not have the drugs listed as most effective in self-deliverance but do have enough sleeping pills to ensure two hours of sleep.

For effective death from drugs in (b), the use of a plastic bag is essential. Death from drugs in (a) is nearly always certain so long as they are taken correctly; I would still also use a plastic bag to make absolutely certain.

The most important factor in bringing about a quick and certain death is the rate of absorption of the drug and how it is introduced into the body. For example, absorption would be different following an intravenous introduction—as opposed to taking the drug orally.

For the drug to be absorbed when it is taken by mouth, it must first dissolve in the body into a solution and then pass into the bloodstream. The stomach has a poor blood supply compared to the rest of the gastrointestinal tract. Thus when there is food in the stomach, any drugs will be held there and cause a delay before they reach the small intestine.

When there is little or no food in the stomach, the valve between it and the small intestine typically opens about three times a minute. On the other hand, when there is a lot of food present, the stomach senses that there is solid matter and the muscle remains shut until the contents liquefy.

The faster the drugs get into the small intestine, with its larger blood supply, the quicker their effect. There will be a massive assault on the central nervous system and the patient will die.

Drinking alcohol along with the drugs will hasten their effect considerably because the drugs will dissolve quickly. Experts say that the alcohol can enhance the effect of some drugs by 50 percent.

Not only is speed required internally to achieve rapid death but the ingestion by mouth must be fast. In cases of failure that I have studied, the patient usually fell asleep before taking a sufficiently lethal dose. Once a person is asleep, drugs can only be given intravenously or by suppository. The exact drugs needed may either not be available or the caregiver may not know how to inject or may not wish to go to that extreme extent in helping.

A person wanting self-deliverance must bolt the drugs. This is best achieved, in my view, by taking them different ways. First take a few tablets of the lethal dose with alcohol, then put the rest into a pudding, or yogurt, which must be eaten with alacrity. (To powder the drugs, either empty the plastic capsules, grind the tablets to a powder with a mortar and pestle, or pulverize them in a blender.)

Thus, the steps to take are:

1. An hour beforehand have an extremely light meal—perhaps tea and a piece of toast—so that the stomach is nearly vacant but not so empty that you would feel nauseous and weak.

2. At the same time take a travel sickness pill such as Dramamine which will ward off nausea later.

3. When the hour has elapsed, take about ten

of your chosen tablets or capsules with as large a drink of spirits or wine as you are comfortable with. Vodka is extremely effective. If you cannot drink alcohol, use your favorite soda drink.

4. Have the additional powdered tablets already mixed into a pudding and swallow that as fast as is possible.

5. Throughout, keep plenty of alcoholic drink or soda at your side to wash this all down. It will also help to dilute the bitter taste.

In both the cases in which I assisted death, the persons fell asleep within a couple of minutes and remained inactive. I have heard from the Netherlands that, in rare cases, the person will speak or their eyes will open during that last sleep. Observers present should expect to hear heavy breathing and probably snoring. This may not be pleasant, but it is a sure sign that the toxicity of the drugs is taking effect.

If the intention is to let the authorities know that this was self-deliverance, leave the empty drug container nearby so that the police or coroner can easily know what was taken. This may eliminate the need for an autopsy or a partial autopsy.

If I ever need to end my own life because of terminal suffering, whether I employed the most potent drugs or the less so, I would still use the plastic bag technique. If you are repulsed by the addition of the plastic bag, then you must accept a 10 percent chance that by some quirk you will wake up, and will have to try again. With the bag, it is 100 percent certain.

Pacemakers

Some people who are fitted with internal heart pacemakers wonder if the gadget will prevent or prolong their dying. It will not prevent dying because pacemakers serve only to maintain steady rhythm of the heart. Once the heart is deprived of blood and oxygen it will stop regardless of the electrical impulses.

Donating Organs

Many people would like to donate their organs or eyes to medical science so that others may be helped to live. The frequently asked question is whether taking one's own life complicates, or eliminates that possibility. There is no easy answer because cases and needs differ so much.

Here is a statement by The Living Bank, a leading organ donor registry (Box 6725, Houston, TX 77265), on the subject:

"The question of age and ability to donate is a concern for many who are considering organ donation.

"Age is not a factor in becoming a member of The Living Bank. Membership is open to anyone who desires to donate their organs and tissue. The Living Bank makes no medical judgments as to the acceptability of any organs. That decision is made by the medical experts. The condition of the organs and tissue is more of a factor in determining viability than the chronological age.

"So you see, you offer a valuable gift regardless of age. Your age should not dissuade you from fulfilling your desire to help others. By your donation, you are indeed a giver of life."

CHAPTER TWENTY-THREE

A Checklist

If you are now comfortable with the decision to die because of the advanced and unbearable state of your terminal illness, and have considered those problems raised in this book which relate to your circumstances, you should review the following list:

1. Be sure that you are in a hopeless condition. Is your judgment clouded by the drugs you are taking? Talk it over with your doctors one more time.

2. Are you just depressed? Should you ask your friends if they think so, or should you ask to see a psychologist or psychiatrist? Depression is usually treatable.

3. If the urge to die is coming from physical pain, ask for pain medications to be increased. If asking is not succeeding, then insist. Be noisy.

4. How much longer can you take the pain (physical and psychic)? Are you communicating well with your medical advisors?

5. Are there other medical options still open to you, or are you willing to forgo them?

6. Are you so near to death anyway that you can handle the situation until the end comes?

7. Will your doctor help you die? He or she might. Is it worth trying? Negotiate frankly but diplomatically. You must respect a physician's decision if he or she refuses.

8. Do this in your home if you can. Check yourself out of the hospital if it is physically possible. A hospital cannot forcibly keep you, but it may require you to sign a release in which you accept responsibility for whatever happens.

9. Give cautious advance warning to those family and friends close to you that you plan, sometime in the near future, to end your life because of your suffering. Do not disclose the planned actual time except to those who will be beside you.

10. Who among those close to you will be hurt by your death now, as opposed to later on? Is this decision yours alone to make?

11. Given that you are already near death, what is it that you fear most, or seek to avoid?

12. If you are a believer in afterlife, is your god willing to accept your suicide as a justifiable escape from terminal suffering? Or are the theologians right that the suffering which often precedes dying is preparation for life in heaven?

13. Make sure you have absolute privacy for up to eight hours. A Friday or Saturday night is usually the quietest time; there are generally no business transactions until Monday.

14. If you have someone beside you during your self-deliverance, to avoid risk of prosecution remind the assister to not touch you before death

and to be discreet in speaking to anyone afterward.

15. Leave a note of explanation as to why you are ending your life, together with your Living Will documents.

16. Make sure that a Will dealing with your financial affairs is with your executor.

17. Consider whether there are any life insurance policies which will be affected by the manner of your death. Leave them where they can be easily found.

18. Leave instructions about disposal of your body, whether you want burial or cremation. Leave guidance on the funeral or memorial service, if any.

19. Tell those around you the complimentary things which have been left unsaid due to the strain of illness. The appropriate "I am grateful for what you've done" or similar remark will help comfort those left behind after you have gone.

20. Be careful about the contents of your stomach.

21. Make sure you have not built up a tolerance to any medication that you are taking regularly. If possible, stop using any regular medications and allow time for your system to clear, probably several days.

22. Do not take the telephone off the hook or disconnect an answering machine. Any changes will only alert callers to something unusual happening. Turn the bell down or put a blanket over the telephone if you do not want to hear it.

23. Make the preparations for your end extremely carefully and with consideration for others. Leave nothing to chance.

. . . and you probably have some very special questions and preparations of your own.

Drug Dosage Table for Use in Self-deliverance from a Terminal Illness

Generic Name	Trade Name	Lethal Dose	Toxicity[3]	Number Tablets × Usual Size
Amobarbital	Amytal, Amal (Australia), Eunoctal (France), Etamyl (Italy), Stadadorm (Germany), Tuinal—in combination with Seconal	4.5 grams*	5	90 × 50 mg.
Butabarbital (Secbutobarbitone)	Butisol, Ethnor (Australia)	3.0 grams	5	100 × 30 mg.
Codeine[4]	In combination with aspirin (Empirin Compound No. I to IV), with Tylenol (Tylenol Compound No. I to IV)	2.4 grams	5	80 × 30 mg.

*1 gram = 1,000 milligrams
You must check the footnotes on pages 127–130

120

Diazepam[1]	Valium, Apozepam (Sweden), Aliseum (Italy), Ducene (Australia)	500 mg. or more	4	100 × 5 mg.

You must check the footnotes on pages 127–130

Generic Name	Trade Name	Lethal Dose	Toxicity[3]	Number Tablets × Usual Size
Flurazepam[1]	Dalmane, Dalmadorm (Denmark), Niotal (Belgium)	3.0 grams	4	100 × 30 mg.
Glutethimide[1]	Doriden, Doridene (Belgium), Glimid (Poland)	24 grams	4	48 × 500 mg.
Chloral Hydrate[1]	Noctec, Chloratex (Canada), Somnox (Belgium)	10 grams or more	4	20 × 500 mg.
Hydromorphone[4]	Dilaudid, Pentagone (Canada)	100–200 mg.	5	50 × 2 mg. or 25 × 4 mg.

You must check the footnotes on pages 127–130

Meprobamate[1]	Miltown, Equanil	45 grams	3	112 × 400 mg.
Methyprylon[1]	Noludar	15 grams	3	50 × 300 mg.
Meperidine[4] (Pethidine)	Demerol, Dolantin (Germany)	3.6 grams	5	72 × 50 mg. or 36 × 100 mg.
Methadone[4]	Dolophine, Adanon	300 mg.	5	60 × 5 mg.
Morphine[4]		200 mg.	5	14 × 15 mg. or 7 × 30 mg.
Orphenadrine[5]	*See note 5. Use only in combination with barbiturates.*	3 grams	—	Powder

You must check the footnotes on pages 127–130

Phenobarbital[1]	Luminal, Gardenal (Canada), Fenical (Spain)	4.5 grams	4	150 × 30 mg. or 75 × 65 mg. or 40 × 100 mg.

You must check the footnotes on pages 127–130

Generic Name	Trade Name	Lethal Dose	Toxicity[3]	Number Tablets × Usual Size
Secobarbital (Quinalbarbitone)	Seconal, Immenox (Italy), Dormona (Switzerland), Secogen, Seral (Canada), Vesperax (Holland, Switzerland) in combination with Brallobarbital	4.5 grams	4	45 × 100 mg.
Propoxyphene[2]	Darvon, Dolotard (Sweden), Abalgin (Denmark), Antalvic (France), Depronal (Holland). Do not confuse with Darvocet.	2.0 grams	5	30 × 65 mg.

You must check the footnotes on pages 127–130

| Pentobarbital | Nembutal (Carbrital if in combination with pentobarbital). | 3.0 grams | 5 | 30 × 100 mg. |

You must check the footnotes on pages 127–130

Footnotes to Drug Dosage Table

1. These drugs may be useful when used with other more potent drugs or with alcohol. They are not recommended for sole use unless no alternative drug is available.
2. This drug is reported to cause death in overdose sometimes within one hour of ingestion. Since it is not a sleeping agent it probably should be combined with one if available. Use only plain propoxyphene, not a compound such as Darvocet.
3. As reported in *Clinical Toxicology of Commercial Products*, category 3 means the drug is rated moderately toxic, category 4 means very toxic, category 5 means extremely toxic.

The ingestion of alcohol along with these drugs multiplies the toxicity by about 50 percent. Drugs in the table marked by a (1) become much more toxic when taken with alcohol. Combinations of drugs will usually enhance toxicity. For instance, sleeping pills (secobarbital) with narcotics (meperidine). Antihistamines, i.e., Benadryl; or phenothiazines, i.e., Compazine or Thorazine also greatly increase the effects of narcotics or sleeping pills and are often prescribed by physicians for that same purpose.
4. Tolerance to effects of narcotic drugs tends to increase dosage requirements. Morphine, methadone, and hydromorphine have minimal effect

when taken orally in most cases, especially if the patient is already using morphine-based drugs for pain. Intravenous administration, or oral administration in combination with barbiturates, may kill a patient.

5. Do not consider Norgesic, Norgesic Forte, Norflex-Plus or generics because they are a combination of Orphenadrine and less toxic drugs. Norflex (3M) is controlled-release and too slow-acting for self-deliverance. Use only Orphenadrine in powder form in combination with barbiturates.

Additional Notes, by a Pharmacist:

(A) Research has indicated that Valium by itself is unlikely to be lethal in any reasonable quantity. If combined with alcohol, barbiturates, or narcotics, it may be lethal. There are no reports of death due to Valium unless it was taken in combination with some other medication. Alcohol comes under the term medication because it is certainly a drug.

(B) Certain other drugs, like antihistamines and tranquilizers, require extremely large doses in order to be fatal. The so-called pain reliever propoxyphene (Darvon) has never been proven to be any better at relieving pain than plain aspirin. But, toxicity-wise, it is completely different in that it has killed many people from overdose and does so quite speedily.

(C) Although one might think that the European names of drugs would be the same as the American names, it is far from the actual case. Included in the preceding Table are certain trade names used in various countries. Some drugs have only a few European names but others, diazepam (Valium) for instance, have a dozen-odd names. The generic (or nontrade) names of most drugs are almost universally the same.

References

Handbook of Poisoning, Robert H. Dreisbach, 1980, Lange Medical Publications, Los Altos, CA.

Clinical Toxicology of Commercial Products, 1976, Williams and Wilkins Company, Baltimore.

The Extra Pharmacopoeia, Ed. William Martindale, 28th edition, The Pharmaceutical Press, 1982, London.

Advice

If you are considering taking your life because you are unhappy, cannot cope, or are confused, please do not use this Table but contact a Crisis Intervention Center or Suicide Prevention Center. (Look in the telephone book. It may be under "Hot Lines." There is a list in the back of this book.) An unfinished life is a terrible thing to waste. This information is meant for consideration only by a *mature adult who is dying* and wishes to know about self-deliverance.

Other Drugs

Cyanide is specifically not recommended for graceful self-deliverance from an advanced terminal illness because the dying can be painful and violent. Similarly, other drugs on the market could be lethal if taken in overdose but the distressing side effects these produce, and the extended length of time they require to take effect, disqualify them from consideration for dignified autoeuthanasia.

No-No's

The following commonly used drugs are not suitable for self-deliverance because they lack toxicity or take too long to act: Halcion, Darvocet-N, Restoril, insulin, Dalmane, aspirin, and acetaminophen.

Best Drugs

All experts on euthanasia agree that the most effective drugs for self-deliverance from a terminal illness are: Seconal, Tuinal, Amytal, and Nembutal. Because they are so lethal they are the hardest to obtain, but do not believe doctors or pharmacists who tell you they are no longer manufactured.

PART 2

Euthanasia Involving Doctors and Nurses

CHAPTER ONE

Justifiable Euthanasia

A great many doctors believe in justified euthanasia but, given the criminal risk, say nothing about it. There are only a handful of America's half-million physicians who have publicly acknowledged their belief in the ethical rightness of aid-in-dying. To acknowledge their belief publicly offers a risk of being branded—and perhaps investigated—as a practitioner of this compassionate option.

Since 1978 I have spoken—by invitation only—to several hundred meetings of medical men and women. Usually I am invited because their patients have been asking awkward questions about help with death. As a rule, after my talk, statements and questions come almost exclusively from opponents and doubters. Supporters remain silent, presumably because of fear of internal political problems. Then, during the coffee break, a man or woman will say to me privately that they agree with my views. "It goes on, anyway," they invariably add. In the next few days I am apt to get supportive notes in the mail from a few others.

Those doctors at meetings who feel free to speak up because they support the status quo almost always raise two points:

1. They have never (in twenty or forty years) been asked by a patient to be helped to die.

2. There is no need for euthanasia because modern medicine has the answers to unbearable suffering.

My answer to the first point is that patients are not stupid. They can usually detect whether a doctor is likely to sympathize with their intended suicide. Perhaps they put out a feeler through the nursing staff. Or they might be using such subjective criteria as the doctor having a name which sounds Jewish or Irish and concluding that there would be opposition on religious grounds. (The patient might or might not be right.) Usually the patient assesses from the bedside manner whether a certain physician is approachable. The second point, pain control and good nursing, requires a much more detailed answer. Certainly, modern pharmaceutical developments have provided us with wonderful analgesics, which, with shrewd management, control terminal pain in about 90 percent of cases. Having read the little amount of literature available on pain management and attended conferences to listen to world experts, my conclusion is that there is about 10 percent of pain that is not yet controllable. We have to care about those people who fall within that margin. It could be me or you.

But even more important than that 10 percent are the other forms of suffering which are not physically painful. I am left with a very distinct and uncomfortable impression that most doctors do not fully appreciate the symptoms of terminal illness that a patient is feeling. Even if they do appreciate them, can they do much about them? Probably not. This is what may be propelling the patient toward a request to be helped to die and thus deserves respect.

Medical Reasons to Help

Not being a doctor or nurse, I do not attempt to teach medicine. However, the matter of patient discomfort and distress is so important and so often downplayed that some of the reasons for those conditions are worth listing:

● Sleeplessness in patients who suffer fatigue, pain, and shortness of breath will cause exhaustion.

● Shortness of breath and labored breath is not infrequent in the terminal phase.

● Fatigue causes the patient to become entirely dependent on day and night nursing.

● Nausea and vomiting can be side effects of drugs or the illness. Vomiting tires, disorients, and degrades the patient.

● Incontinence is humanly degrading to the personal dignity of the patient who it forces even more into the intimate care of others.

● Excessive salivation caused by blockage of the throat means constant spitting which is wearisome and depressing.

● Thirst.

● Bedsores in patients who are difficult to move, especially if they are heavily built.

● Perspiration.

- Hunger.
- Coughing.
- Fungal infections of the mouth.
- Constipation, especially that which is caused by drugs containing morphine or other narcotics.
- Itching, which is worse with jaundice.
- Infections from catheters.
- Dependence on others, especially in people who were previously totally self-reliant.
- Hiccups.
- Weight loss.
- Loss of dignity which may accompany confusion, disorientation, forgetfulness, and other behavioral or intellectual changes so common in the terminal stages of so many illnesses.

Any one of these problems which persists can become unbearable to a patient who may already be depressed at the prospect of dying, leaving loved ones, having unfulfilled dreams, and losing material possessions. In addition to grief, probably a dying patient's biggest fear may be that things are going to get worse before the end comes. This anxiety may be present, despite reassurances, from the moment a terminal diagnosis was revealed.

Caring health professionals should seek not only to relieve these and other special discomforts and anxieties but must take them into consideration when asked by a patient for euthanasia.

Professional Reasons to Help

There are plenty of reasons why a physician should help a suffering terminally ill patient to die. Here are some of them:

● Physicians know better than anyone else approximately when the patient will die, and the manner of death. If the patient is asking for euthanasia and it clearly is not justified, or is too early, the physician is in the best position to advance arguments to this effect.

● Only physicians have lawful access to lethal drugs, know the techniques for their administration, and can avoid toxicological mistakes caused by tolerance and interaction.

● Physicians are trained to observe criteria before acting. The Dutch experience has shown careful procedures and preparations are essential in acts of euthanasia.

● Certain patients, such as those with ALS or cancer of the throat, cannot swallow and need skillful injections to end life.

Social Reasons to Help

● By the time the end of life is reached, some people have no one to assist them to die. Widows have often outlived their close relatives and friends, for instance.

● Sometimes relatives of the patient have too many emotional problems to be able to help. Issues of guilt, unfinished business, even financial debt, may confuse the person to whom the patient is turning for assistance.

● The patient is certain to be afraid of doing it

alone for fear of botching it, then having to live on with the stigma and perhaps physical damage.

● The role of the physician is both to cure and to relieve suffering. When cure is no longer possible and the patient seeks relief through euthanasia, the help of physicians is most appropriate.

● Alone at this crucial time, the physician is the independent broker, the one not involved emotionally or historically, and possessing the technology and skill to end the patient's life with certainty and gentleness. It has to be a carefully negotiated death, with both patient and doctor sharing the responsibilities it entails.

Reasons Not to Help

It would be judicious and fair for a physician to decline to help if one or more of the following circumstances prevails:

● Helping another person to die offends the physician's moral and ethical codes.

● The physician hardly knows the patient and/or mutual respect is lacking.

● The physician is not fully conversant with the patient's medical status. This is not the time for hasty, ill-considered actions which may be regretted later.

● There remain other treatments which offer a positive chance of recovery or remission. (But this is hardly the time to think about experimental medicine.) The patient has the right of ultimate choice so long as it is an informed decision.

● The patient who is asking for assistance in suicide is clearly depressed and so not rational. That

138

depression may be treatable. Bear in mind that the prospect of death would throw most people into the doldrums, so first wait and see if it passes. If not, treat it with appropriate drugs and also check to see if some other circumstances, such as family stress or financial worries, are causing the unhappiness. If doubt remains about the patient's rationality, after getting consent, call in a psychologist or psychiatrist for an evaluation.

In a lengthy and thought-provoking article in the *New England Journal of Medicine* (3/30/89) by twelve distinguished American doctors, ten of them were bold enough to say ". . . it is not immoral for a physician to assist in the rational suicide of a terminally ill person."

I admire this pithy summing up of the situation by Dr. Daniel D. Federman, Dean of Medical Education at Harvard University: "If the patient is not depressed (as opposed to sad, angry, or appropriately hopeless), if his or her judgment is not clouded by drugs or the disease process, if he or she is fully informed with state-of-the-art [medical] data, and if the decision to terminate life is in proportion to the amount and quality that remain, then there are circumstances in which suicide can be deemed rational and in which a doctor could properly agree to make it easier. . . . In the very restricted domain that I've described, I believe a physician *may* morally choose to assist the suicide of a terminally ill patient but is not *required* to do so." (*Harvard Health Letter*, Vol. 16, No. 10, August 1991)

CHAPTER TWO

A Doctor's Suicide Machine

On June 4, 1990, Dr. Jack Kevorkian took an action which profoundly shook the medical profession and news of it reverberated around the world: he helped a woman commit suicide and the next day talked freely about it in *The New York Times.* The woman was in the early stages of Alzheimer's disease but was not his patient.

A controversy of unprecedented proportions for the subject of euthanasia was touched off. The public was generally supportive of Dr. Kevorkian; the media courted him assiduously for two months; and the medical and psychiatric professions were thrown into confusion, issuing conflicting statements of condemnation and support.

The Patient

Janet Adkins was a 54-year-old, happily married mother of three grown sons—who a year earlier had been diagnosed with Alzheimer's, a degenerative disease of the brain. Prior to its discovery she had joined the Hemlock Society. A physically and intellectually active woman, Mrs. Adkins was horrified as the illness began to affect her faculties and, with her husband's consent, resolved to end her life before the symptoms became more serious. She had received all known medical treatments for the condition, even some experimental.

She approached three doctors in the vicinity of Portland, Oregon, where she lived, and asked them to help her to die. Two of the doctors were members of the Hemlock Society. At different times, the whole family counseled with a skilled family therapist. This care continued up to one week before her death. "Both Mrs. Adkins and the rest of the family were at peace with her decision to die at the time of her choosing," the therapist, Myriam Coppens, subsequently told me.

Mrs. Adkins believed in God, and attended the Unitarian Universalist Church. She had told her minister of her plan to die soon.

None of the three doctors would directly help her die despite their obvious sympathy with euthanasia. She wanted one of them to administer the drugs in her possession because, like so many people in the same situation, she feared a mistake. Their reasons for refusing to help appear to have been that (1) she was not their patient; (2) the risk of prosecution was too great.

One of the doctors has told me that during his career he has helped six people to die with drugs. Each was a respected patient who had asked to die in justifiable medical circumstances.

Janet Adkins heard about Dr. Kevorkian through the media in late 1989. She even saw his machine and its workings explained on the *Donahue* show. Like thousands of other people in her situation, she wanted a gentle and certain death with dignity and this was what Dr. Kevorkian was offering. She made contact with him and he suggested she come when she was ready.

Dr. Kevorkian graduated from the University of Michigan Medical School in 1952 as an outstanding student, and took further training in pathology. He is an accomplished musician and painter. Dr. Kevorkian worked in hospitals in Michigan and California and always showed a deep interest in different aspects of the death process.

He occasionally transfused blood from recently dead people for use in the living, and made a special study of the retinas of people in an attempt to discover when the point of death is irreversible. In 1958 he was asked to leave his appointment in pathology at an Ann Arbor hospital because he wanted to persuade men condemned to death for murder in Ohio to volunteer for medical experiments. After years of seeking a publisher in 1986, a foreign journal printed his paper on the possible medical benefits of human experimentation on condemned prisoners.

Dr. Kevorkian approached the Hemlock Society in 1988 with an idea to open a suicide clinic in southern California to which Hemlock would refer terminal people who wanted to die. He argued that not only was this necessary for humanity but, if he was prosecuted for assisting suicides, as seemed likely, the resulting publicity would benefit the euthanasia cause. At that time a sister group of Hemlock was battling to qualify *The*

Death with Dignity Act for the ballot in California. (It failed through weak organization to get sufficient signatures.)

I suggested to Dr. Kevorkian that since the campaign in which the euthanasia movement was at that point engaged to legitimize physician aid-in-dying for the terminally ill, any law-breaking would be bad publicity. He reluctantly accepted my arguments.

Dr. Kevorkian ceased to practice medicine in 1988, but still retained his license. His controversial views made it extremely difficult for him to get a hospital appointment. Ostracized by the medical profession, he printed a business card which read: *Jack Kevorkian, M.D., Bioethics and Obiatry. Special death counseling.* (Dr. Kevorkian defines "obiatry" as going to your death with the aid of a doctor.)

Late in 1989 when he publicly announced his invention of a suicide machine, the media showed interest for a couple of weeks. Many members of the public were spellbound. Some who were sick saw him as the new messiah and scores contacted him about helping them. Mrs. Adkins sent him her medical records.

The Site and the Interview

Mrs. Adkins and her husband flew two thousand miles from Portland, Oregon, to Royal Oak, Michigan, to meet Dr. Kevorkian in person the day before her death. That interview, which Dr. Kevorkian shrewdly videotaped, convinced him that she was rational. For weeks previously Dr.

Kevorkian had searched for a suitable place for the procedure to be carried out. The local funeral home, offices, motels, and churches all refused him use of their premises, as did members of the Hemlock Society when asked if he could use their homes. Why he did not use his own apartment is unclear.

The end came in Dr. Kevorkian's 1968 Volkswagen van in a campsite lot in Grovelands, Oakland County, Michigan. He had installed curtains for privacy. Mrs. Adkins refused to let her husband of thirty-four years be present at her death, so he remained in a nearby motel until informed that the end had come.

The Suicide Machine

Dr. Kevorkian constructed a small frame of aluminum scrap from which he suspended three inverted bottles. One contained a saline solution, the second sodium pentothal, and the third a solution of potassium chloride and succinylcholine. A small electric motor from a toy car powered the intravenous lines.

The steps to death were as follows:

1. Mrs. Adkins was hooked up intravenously to the harmless saline solution.

2. Her heart was monitored by cardiograph electrodes on her arms and legs.

3. When Mrs. Adkins was ready to die, she pushed a button that caused a valve to shut off the saline solution and open the adjoining line of pentothal (thiopental). This drug put her to sleep within about thirty seconds.

4. A timing device connected to the line between the second and third containers triggered after one minute. The potassium chloride and the succinylcholine (a muscle relaxant) began to flow into the arm of the now unconscious woman. Death occurred within six minutes.

Dr. Kevorkian informed the medical examiner's office, the husband, and *The New York Times*, which devoted most of its front page to the story the next day.

The Law

Dr. Kevorkian knew that Michigan, his home state, has the most ambiguous laws on assisted suicide in the United States, with cases ranging from an extremely punitive sentence, to freedom. The first known prosecution in America for euthanasia came in Michigan in 1920 when Frank Roberts assisted his wife's suicide. She had multiple sclerosis and had attempted suicide before. At her urging Mr. Roberts mixed Paris Green (containing arsenic) with water, put it within her reach, and she drank it. Convicted of first-degree murder, he received life imprisonment with hard labor and, while his case, *People* v. *Roberts*, went into the legal history books, he was never heard of again and presumably died in prison.

The pendulum swung the other way in 1983 when a young man, Steven Paul Campbell, was convicted of first-degree murder by leaving a gun and ammunition with a friend, who used it to commit suicide. The deceased had been depressed and was drinking heavily. Campbell walked free when the Michigan Court of Appeals pronounced: "The legislature has not defined aiding a suicide as a crime. Aiding a suicide does not fall within any definitions of homicide."

But Michigan law enforcement authorities moved quickly to stop Dr. Kevorkian. They asked a court for a temporary restraining order, by which they impounded his vehicle, the machine, and his drugs. The court also issued an order forbidding him to help anybody else.

Part of the official "complaint" against him was that "it is likely other candidates for his 'machine' will be turning up." In fact, he was swamped with inquiries but refrained from building another machine.

The publicity over the Kevorkian-Adkins affair indirectly led within two months to a murder charge against a California man, Robert Bertram Harper, for assisting his wife in committing suicide in a motel in Wayne County, the next county to Kevorkian's. Virginia Harper, suffering from extensive cancer, had a powerful desire to end her life in the presence of her husband and daughter, chiefly so that she would not botch it as she had done a year earlier when acting alone.

The threesome flew two thousand miles from Sacramento to Michigan and checked into a motel in Romulus, near Detroit. A few hours later Mrs. Harper attempted suicide by swallowing ten Dalmane intended to put her to sleep, followed by a plastic bag which she pulled over her head. Probably because of jet lag, a violent thunderstorm, tension in a strange and overheated motel room, sleep did not come and she repeatedly pulled off the plastic bag. Eventually her husband and daughter calmed her and—this was his legal mistake—Bob Harper gently put the plastic bag over his wife's head and secured it around her neck with elastic bands. She lay quietly and expired as she had wished.

Having read the case of *People v. Campbell*, and been influenced by the recent rumpus over Dr. Kevorkian, Mr. Harper told the state police everything, believing he had not committed a crime. He was arrested and charged with first-degree murder due to the prosecuting attorney's reliance on his admission that he had *provided physical assistance* in his wife's death by helping her don the plastic bag. The next day the district attorney's office issued a press statement saying that it was a great mistake for people to think they could come to Michigan to assist suicide, a statement which indicated that, to some degree, Mr. Harper was being used as a deterrent example.

Six months after Janet Adkins's death, Dr. Kevorkian, too, was charged with murder. Ten days later a judge dismissed the charge as insupportable. The Hemlock Society arranged Mr. Harper's defense, and I was one of the witnesses at the four-day trial in Detroit which ended in an acquittal by the jury on May 10, 1991. The prosecution sought a second-degree murder conviction, without prison time, but the jury took only an hour to free Mr. Harper.

Ethical Consequences

Articles and letters in newspapers and magazines indicate that most physicians opposed Dr. Kevorkian's action. A brave few supported him. It is my belief based on experience that a great many more were too nervous about their own professional positions to declare support. It requires courage and a secure financial situation for the average doctor to come out in favor of what is at present a possibly criminal action. (Most experts believe that Dr. Kevorkian would have been charged with murder the next day in any state other than Michigan where the law is fuzzy.)

Religious leaders condemned Dr. Kevorkian. "Any such thing as a suicide machine is a moral abomination," said a spokesman for the Archdiocese of Detroit. "God alone is the author of life, from beginning to end." Mrs. Adkins's own church, the Unitarian, defended her right to act according to her circumstances and conscience.

Some doctors considered Dr. Kevorkian's use of a machine which had a gadget to pass control from physician to patient to be an ethical cop-out. Said one: "Even if he gets off the hook legally, there is a moral accountability that cannot be ignored." A few months later the Michigan State Medical Society Board of Directors took much the same line. "We don't think an individual physician can arbitrarily decide that euthanasia is legally and morally correct," it stated. "But giving someone a medicine or allowing them to take a medicine is not necessarily different than stopping

148

chemotherapy or stopping antibiotics." The medical society declined to condemn the "suicide machine" and made no recommendation to remove his medical license, something which would certainly have happened years ago (*Ann Arbor News*, 9/21/90).

The Hemlock Society approved of Dr. Kevorkian helping Mrs. Adkins to die because it knew first-hand that she had been contemplating this for at least six months, had been refused help by other doctors, and her family was in psychological counseling. "But it is hardly death with dignity to have to travel two thousand miles and die in the back of a van in a campsite lot," said Hemlock. "We need to change the law so that this sort of compassionate help by a doctor can happen at home or in the hospital."

Dr. Kevorkian fought back powerfully against his critics, saying that he would help more people to die as soon as he had cleared up legal problems. But he appeared to be having doubts about how physician-assisted suicide should be conducted. Three months after his challenge to the medical profession's indecision over euthanasia, he told the *Detroit News* his plan: "If a terminally ill person wanted to die, I would go to their home and consult with them, their family, their minister, and all the relevant doctors. I would lay out the procedure and then the doctors would determine if the case qualifies for what the person wants. A decision would then be made by the specially appointed panel."

These criteria did not relate in any way to what he had done with Mrs. Adkins. Nor did they square with his other professed intention of starting suicide centers across America. The Hemlock Society found itself opposing Dr. Kevorkian on this, arguing that suicide centers were unnecessary because, with a simple change of the law through *The Death with Dignity Act*, help with death could happen quietly at home or at the hospital as a privately negotiated arrangement between doctor and patient. Additionally, there could never be enough suicide centers across America within easy distance of people sick and unable to travel.

Finally, Hemlock argued that such centers could be a cause of massive abuse unless heavily regulated.

Moreover, the prospect of patients being obliged to hand over life-or-death decisions to a panel of doctors is not appealing to most euthanasia supporters, who prefer to make their own quality of life decisions and then elicit the discreet and lawful support of the treating physician.

A considerable amount of the controversy centered on whether Mrs. Adkins was terminal and whether she had taken her life too soon. She was criticized posthumously for committing suicide a few days after playing tennis with one of her sons, a comment which ignored the fact that she could no longer keep the score. What drove Mrs. Adkins to her self-destruction was that her mind was undoubtedly weakening, and she knew it was going to get much worse within the next two years.

Is Alzheimer's disease a terminal illness? Some say not. Others point out that as it is incurable and death follows from other illnesses which attack the weakened body, it deserves to be classed as a "terminal illness." Alzheimer's is not alone as a disease which kills its victims by indirect means. The public's dread of Alzheimer's stems from the knowledge that the illness will take five or ten years to run its course, putting a dreadful burden on the family. Alzheimer's can be seen as a form of "mind death" or "partial brain death."

While Dr. Kevorkian drew huge quantities of both praise and criticism, he undoubtedly performed a notable public service by forcing the medical profession to rethink its attitude on euthanasia. The Hemlock Society and others have been arguing for years that there is a better way than self-deliverance or covert physician assisted suicide.

In October 1991, Dr. Kevorkian helped two more women to die and this time did not receive the same sympathetic consideration as on the first occasion. Neither woman could be definitely described as "terminally ill" although there is no doubt that they were suffering considerably from their illnesses and wished to die. (One woman had serious multiple sclerosis and the other constant pelvic pain.)

The deaths took place in a holiday cabin in Michigan, one woman using the suicide machine, while the other, because her veins were hard to find, died by breathing carbon monoxide through a mask.

Dr. Kevorkian's action on this occasion was in defiance of a local civil court restraining order telling him not to repeat his assistance of suicide. Almost immediately the Michigan State Medical Society, which had seemed tolerant of his first action, withdrew his license to practice medicine.

Michigan law enforcement authorities carried out extensive investigations into the two deaths, and in February 1992, Dr. Kevorkian was ordered to stand trial for two murders. He maintained that the deaths were voluntary-assisted suicides for medical reasons and that he had broken no laws. I agree with him, because murder means robbing a person of a life they wish to keep; these two women wished to die.

Many people in the euthanasia movement felt that Dr. Kevorkian's second- and third-assisted suicides, coming as they did two weeks before the world's first vote of electors in Washington state on a new law permitting physician-assisted death for the dying upon request, did their cause great harm. The specter of maverick doctors moving to Washington to help people to die in curious circumstances was raised and—for whatever reason —the law reform which had been expected to pass, was narrowly defeated by 54 percent of the vote to 46 percent. If more stringent regulations governing physicians had been written into the proposed Washington law, as they are in California's, I think it would have passed.

Dr. Kevorkian is well-intentioned but he is moving too far, too fast, in a field of medical law and ethics in which we must first tackle the bigger problem of helping the terminally ill to die. Although a few doctors had supported his helping the first woman, Janet Adkins, to die, support for the aided deaths of the second and third women was noticeably lacking, even from the progressive wing of the medical profession.

And so began an important debate between the public and the medical profession: What is suffering? Are doctors sufficiently aware of the psychic pain that accompanies serious illness?

CHAPTER THREE

EuTHANASia by Physicians

Increasingly physicians are being asked to perform active euthanasia for dying patients. The following chapters are intended to help doctors and nurses carry out this sensitive and responsible procedure with confidence and skill.

The criteria under which dying patients ought to be considered for euthanasia are broadly:

1. The patient is making a consistent and persistent request for help with death because of suffering that is unbearable. The underlying cause must be terminal physical illness, but the psychological effects of that condition are also an important consideration. For everybody's peace of mind, these requests by the patient must be confirmed in writing and the signature witnessed.

2. Two doctors agree that the patient is likely to die (within reasonable medical judgment) in the next few months. This agreement should also be in writing.

3. The patient fully understands his or her condition and has been made aware of all medical options, including hospice care.

4. Family members have been informed of the patient's request and their views have been con-

sidered. No member of the family, nor the family as a group, can authorize euthanasia or veto it.

5. The timing of the death is exclusively in the hands of the patient and revocation can be made, orally or in writing, at any point. Immediately before causing death, the doctor must, in the presence of a witness, ask the patient if this is still desired.

6. Only a qualified physician may cause the death, and in the most humane way known, that is agreeable to the patient.

These criteria are provided for ethical guidance only. Except in the Netherlands, their legality elsewhere is highly doubtful at present. All persons taking part in the act of euthanasia must consider their position with regard to possible criminal liability. So long as the assisted suicide is justifiable in humanitarian terms, and is carried out thoughtfully and discreetly, charges are extremely unlikely. At this time, the climate of public opinion favors such compassion and prosecutors are sensitive to these factors.

There will always be the exceptional case such as when a patient is extremely ill and suffering unbearably, will not recover, but is not terminally ill as we know the term. Alzheimer's disease, advanced multiple sclerosis, ALS are the most likely cases. With such diseases, and some rarer others, the suffering can be unbearable. There is no cure and everybody knows the patient will only get worse. The patient may well ask for death to be hastened. The medical team must then ask itself if it can assist in this case. After a complete review of the circumstances, I believe that it may rightly decide to do so. There can be no standard criteria for some human dilemmas; each case must be considered on its merits.

Home or Hospital?

Where the euthanasia takes place is only important if the patient must, because of the particular symptoms, be kept in the hospital. Ideally, the euthanasia should take place in the patient's home, in the presence of whomever the patient wishes. But whether in the hospital or at home, the assistance in death should be kept to the same high standard of consultation and consideration. In the chapter on nurses and euthanasia I will deal with team aspects of euthanasia for health professionals.

Once the decision to accelerate death has been made, the physician may consult with the pharmacist about the most suitable drug to be used for this particular patient. If the pharmacist has doubts about what is happening, they should be stated and, if he or she is still troubled after discussion, should withdraw from the plan. When the actual drug and dosage are agreed upon, these should be put in writing. Dispensation of the clearly labeled substance should be given directly from the pharmacist into the hands of the physician.

Most physicians have remarkably little knowledge of how to end a life. They are taught the therapeutic value of drugs but not how they may work to end life. In the following chapters I report how Dutch doctors and pharmacists have learned in the past twenty years to do that with the best known scientific means. This is the best source material we have.

While we in the Hemlock Society have garnered considerable knowledge in patient self-deliverance—and the Dutch and others have drawn on that from our books and reports—there has not, because of legal dangers, been the opportunity in America and Britain to publish material on physician aid-in-dying. Where it happens it is covert. The experience is not shared.

Which Drugs Are Best?

The ideal substance is one that brings about quick and painless euthanasia. Exactly which substance to use will depend on whether the patient elects to drink it or be injected, the physical condition of the patient, and the drugs already being used for treatment.

The substance must be one which can be administered intramuscularly and/or intravenously, taken orally, or given by rectal insertion. Since there is no one substance capable of all these uses, many must be considered.

While most patients in the Netherlands prefer the injection method of assistance in dying, some choose "to drink the hemlock" (to use a classical metaphor). Liquid is preferable to tablets or capsules because it is easier to swallow. It is also likely to act faster because it is already dissolved. The disadvantages are the possibility of vomiting or an objectionable taste that makes the liquid undrinkable.

The key to rapid death from a lethal substance taken by mouth lies in the amount of contents of the stomach and intestinal tract. I have discussed this in the chapter on self-deliverance (Chapter 22). Once the substance has been taken, the physician should not leave the patient. If the physician must leave, a nurse should be left in charge. The doctor should return at frequent intervals until death can be certified.

The best combinations of drugs to use for self-administered euthanasia under medical supervision are reported in a later chapter. There are several alternatives for routes by which the drugs are administered but they vary in quality and reliability.

Rectal

This is the least desirable of methods because of the need for an enema and the position the patient must assume. Many patients also have difficulty in retaining the suppository. If used, suppositories with a barbiturate in the form of sodium salt are preferable since they tend to relax the bowels. But the chief disadvantage of suppositories in euthanasia is that provision of an adequate lethal dose is difficult. In addition, absorption into the blood is time-consuming and consequently their potency is diminished. The potential necessity of inserting more suppositories after the patient has become unconscious would undoubtedly be a psychological drawback for the doctor. All considered, this should be the method of last resort.

Intramuscular

The speed with which this method works depends upon the composition of the fluid used and the healthiness of the patient's circulatory system. In this situation the time it takes to end life is difficult to predict. By searching out the area of the body best supplied with blood, giving a deep intramuscular injection into it, and then manually massaging the site, the process of causing death will be considerably speeded up.

Intravenous

An intravenous injection is the ideal method and has a deserved reputation for bringing about swift death. If the patient is already on an intravenous drip that administers analgesia, the lethal substance can probably best be introduced that way.

Subcutaneous

Dutch experts do not consider this method suitable because of difficulties similar to those of intramuscular injection which cannot be overcome by techniques.

How Much?

The volume used depends partly on which of the methods just outlined is used. An oral potion probably requires 100ml; an intramuscular injection 10ml that is best divided into two injection places.

159

How Long?

The lethal substance should produce a deep, irreversible coma within minutes, with a maximum time span of thirty minutes. Death should follow within another thirty minutes or—if taken orally—at most, several hours. In my own experience as an assister, my first wife (bone cancer, age 42) took an oral overdose, passed out immediately, and died within fifty minutes. Eleven years later, when I helped my father-in-law (congestive heart failure, age 92) to die, I was better informed and he died in twenty minutes. In both cases secobarbital was the chief agent.

The most important thing I had learned by observation in the intervening years was that swift ingestion of the overdose is the crucial factor. The central nervous system (CNS) has to be dealt a rapid and fierce blow to produce beneficent euthanasia. This is why an intravenous injection is superior to oral administration.

Side Effects

Whatever pharmaceutical substance is used, it must not cause any undesirable psychological side effects such as depression, pain, anxiety, or hallucinations. Neither must there be physiological problems such as convulsions, tightness of the chest, vomiting, or motor restlessness. Obviously, if there is vomiting then the amount of drug, orally administered, reaching the CNS will be diminished.

Drug Interactions

Whatever drug is used, its interaction with other drugs already being taken by the patient is a most important factor. Some drugs in combination either nullify or enhance each other. Although the permutations are too many to report on here, physicians should be sure to investigate the potential interactions carefully.

CHAPTER FOUR

Nurses on the Frontline

The diagnosis of a patient's condition is the responsibility of the treating physician. Treatment of that condition is the responsibility of both the physician and the patient after the circumstances and the options have been discussed. The desirability of euthanasia is then a matter of a negotiated pact.

Caught on the frontline of the daily care and close involvement with the patient, but having limited responsibility in decision-making, is the nurse. It is quite likely that he or she will hear first about the patient's desire to die. The nurse may or may not sympathize with the request, or may need time to come to terms with it.

If bypassed in the process of decision-making about euthanasia, then not only will the nurse feel ignored and insulted but a valuable source of experience and information will be lost. This could lead to problems. Therefore, it is preferable to have nurses involved in helping a patient to die. However, they should not be asked to decide, nor to administer the lethal drug.

First, a nurse should understand the basic types of euthanasia: passive euthanasia—allowing to die by disconnection of life-support systems (this is legally permissible); active euthanasia—helping to die by administration of a lethal drug (this might be a borderline criminal action until the law forbidding assistance in suicide is changed). Obviously, if the first method will achieve what the patient desires, the second is unnecessary.

Nevertheless, stopping treatment that is pointless, dealing with a patient refusing treatment that might delay death, or managing pain by massive overdoses of drugs that coincidentally hasten death, can produce troubling feelings about euthanasia if they are not shared and dealt with. Discussion among all involved health care professionals of what is happening, or about to happen, is of paramount importance.

The nurse must consider whether the patient is acting under free will and not being pressured by anybody—and whether the patient has carefully considered the situation and knows the options.

If a nurse is aware that the foregoing are in question, then it is a duty to bring this to the attention of the medical team.

Because the nurse is in the patient's presence far longer than anyone else, the input from this source can be vital in assessing the patient's competence and rationality. A nurse with any doubt about the patient's condition and treatment should question the doctor about it but, of course, cannot be held responsible for it. Nurses may be held responsible either for not questioning or for administering questionable treatment even under doctor's orders.

Professionally and legally the doctor alone is responsible for diagnosis. Final decisions on euthanasia (active or passive) should also be the doctor's domain in consultation with at least one other physician. But the views of the attending nurse or nurses should not be ignored.

The patient might wish to deal with the question of euthanasia with the doctor only, not involving the nursing staff. This has to be respected. However, this does not happen often.

The assets that a nurse may bring to a situation of negotiated death include providing information on the patient's family and social situation and, perhaps, acting as the patient's advocate. The nurse might be aware that the patient wishes to try a further medical procedure to relieve suffering, but is afraid to ask the doctor.

When a decision has been made to accede to the patient's wish to die, the entire medical team must know when this will be, and the manner in which it will come. This is especially true if the patient has chosen the oral method for taking the drugs since it can be a lengthy process. While everything must be done to reduce the stress on the medical team, a degree of emotional involvement in the dying of the patient is eminently worthwhile to preserve an appreciation of the inherent sanctity of life.

To summarize, a nurse who wishes to participate in the euthanasia process should become well versed in the ethics and law of euthanasia, particularly as applied in the applicable county, state, professional organization, and institution. To know the rules does not necessarily require obedience if there is an overriding moral imperative.

The nurse should be involved, and be included by colleagues, at all stages of the affair. The nurse must be allowed to make a professional contribution.

CHAPTER FIVE

Euthanasia in Practice

I do not have much time for fancy definitions so common in the medical profession, and their satellite profession, ethics, about what to call the action of helping someone to die. For me, "euthanasia" means the general principle of helping someone have a good death, and "assisted suicide" means the actual action taken to achieve this. So far as a physician is concerned, this action could either be the writing out of a prescription for lethal drugs at the request of a patient who wishes to privately end his or her own life, or the direct administration—orally or intravenously—of lethal drugs to a dying patient.

Euphemistic phrases like "aid-in-dying" and "physician-assisted death" have sprung up in recent years in an attempt to substitute for words like "euthanasia" and "assisted suicide." But let us call a spade a spade and stick to basic language when dealing with a serious subject. In the real world of actually dealing with dying, at all levels of communication I have found that euphemisms and the media's favorite phrases like "mercy killing" and "the right to die" only cause misunderstandings which can have tragic consequences. In this field, good communication between physicians and patients is of paramount importance, so let us use basic language and not be afraid of words like "suicide" if that is really what we are talking about.

True, many people much prefer to substitute "self-deliverance" for "suicide" because that word is so loaded with taboos. As the executive director of a large "right to choose to die" group I felt obliged to go along with this term to a certain extent, but I prefer blunter terms.

Prescription Euthanasia

In some cases, a physician decides to help the dying of a particular patient by writing out a prescription for a lethal dose of drugs. This should only be done if the patient has made out a good case—philosophically, emotionally, and practically—for being able to handle his or her own dying.

Making out a prescription knowing that it will be used for suicide is, technically, a crime almost everywhere. But juries today will not go along with attempts to prosecute in such cases (see the case of Dr. Timothy E. Quill, in Rochester, New York, in 1991), while in the state of New Hampshire there has been a significant attempt in the legislature to change the law to permit "prescription euthanasia" only.

I do not think this is an ideal way to handle the situation, but sometimes the circumstance may call for it in an imperfect world. The patient should be urged to have someone with them during their self-deliverance (or suicide) and some doctors give permission to be telephoned if anything goes wrong. This permission is a great comfort to many people. Usually the only occasion when a call is made from the patient's helper is about the length of time it takes for the drugs to end life; people are in a high state of anxiety and wonder why the drugs do not work more quickly.

From listening to hundreds of accounts over the last fifteen years, there is no doubt in my mind that the only drugs which a doctor should prescribe for a patient's self-deliverance are the barbiturates listed in the drug dosage chart in the center of this book, namely secobarbital (common commercial name Seconal with variations around the world) or pentobarbital (Nembutal) or amobarbital (Amytal or Tuinal).

Careful instructions should be given to the patient about how these are self-administered. The patient should be cautioned that a decision to end their life is entirely their own moral and legal responsibility and should only be taken after the most careful consideration. (See the checklist in Chapter 23 for many of the factors.)

It is advisable to make a firm pact with the patient to maintain silence about where the prescription came from. An added legal precaution might be to make out two or three different prescriptions over a period for the total amount of drugs so that none contains a lethal dose. This way, too, the patient is slowed down from too rapid action, but consider carefully whether or not any such delay is appropriate in each case.

The time is not far off when a physician will feel comfortable writing out such a prescription, and sitting with the patient as the drugs take effect. After all, is that not only good medicine but human compassion and friendship? But we are not yet at that stage of law reform, so physicians must continue to act cautiously to protect themselves.

Direct Euthanasia

Physicians are taught the beneficial effects of drugs and, while they are supposed to also know about their toxicity, they usually do not know much about which drugs end life in the swiftest and most graceful way. I know of one case where a physician carelessly prescribed the MLD (minimum lethal dose) out of a textbook of a barbiturate for a cancer patient who wanted death and, of course, her self-deliverance was botched, much to his chagrin.

Of course there are many drugs in today's huge arsenal of pharmaceuticals which will end life in some fashion. But in euthanasia we are only concerned with those relatively few drugs which end the dying patient's life *rapidly and painlessly.*

Oral

Some patients wish to take the drug themselves in the presence of their physician. In such cases the ideal prescription guidelines might be a dissolved and shaken mixture of:

Pentobarbital sodium	9g
Alcohol	20ml
Purified water	15ml
Propylene glycol	10ml
Orange syrup	50ml

alternatively

Secobarbital sodium	9g
Alcohol	20ml
Purified water	15ml
Propylene glycol	10ml
Orange syrup	50ml

Even with the addition of the syrup, the above potions still have a bitter taste which the patient will be aware of when drinking.

Physicians in the Netherlands, where euthanasia is permitted by the courts under strict regulation, have discovered that Orphenadrine (normally used in the treatment of Parkinson's disease) is highly effective in bringing an end to life when combined with barbiturates. For instance:

Pentobarbital sodium	9g
Orphenadrine hydrochloride	3g
Alcohol	20ml
Propylene glycol	10ml
Purified water	15ml
Orange syrup	50ml

When the patient chooses oral consumption of the lethal drug, consideration must be given to the possibility of vomiting and an antiemetic such as metoclopramide (Primperan or Reglan in the United States) or alizapride (Litican) should be used.

There are also the phenothiazine derivatives such as prochlorperazine (Stemetil or Compazine) and certain other antiemetics which may be suitable to different cases.

Intravenous

Every physician knows that patients treated with narcotic analgesics build up huge tolerance often lasting for years. To use morphine, even in high dosage, on such a patient may produce no more than a stupor.

In nontolerant patients, an intravenous injection of 10mg of morphine hydrochloride will often help a patient who is on the edge to die but will not accelerate the dying process in all cases.

It hardly needs saying that intravenous injection of drugs is by far the speediest and most effective way of ending a dying person's life. But exactly which drug or drugs are used depends very much on the condition of the patient, so precise knowledge on this issue must await the definitive medical textbook sometime in the future. Until then, physicians must use their knowledge and common sense.

But it can be said from present knowledge, emanating mostly from the Netherlands, that an injection of a barbiturate to knock out the central nervous system, followed within a few minutes by a second injection of a curare derivative, should produce a peaceful death within about thirty minutes or less.

In every case the physician should wait near the bedside until death is certain.

A person who has not been taking barbiturates to assist sleep could, for example, die from 1g of sodium thiopental but to avoid the risk of tolerance 1.5 to 2g would be the wiser amount to administer. Such a dosage would induce a coma, after which a muscle relaxant such as alcuronium dichloride and pancuronium dibromide (Pavulon) and also vecuronium bromide (Norcuron) can immediately be used.

Triple the normal therapeutic dose of a muscle relaxant should be used, for example 45mg alcuronium dichloride or 18mg pancuronium dibromide, using a normal anesthetic route.

Today so many drugs come from the pharmaceutical companies to the physician in handy, ready, made-up injectable packs, with the contents and volumes clearly marked, that in each euthanasia case the physician has to make his or her individual calculation about lethal dosage.

The rule of thumb for certain death is to triple the stated minimum lethal dosage. And the bottom-line question physicians must ask themselves before carrying out euthanasia: "Would I want this for myself if I were in this patient's condition?"

Bibliographical Notes

Only three books on self-deliverance and assisted suicide have been published for sale in bookstores and to be available in lending libraries. *Let Me Die Before I Wake*, subtitled "Hemlock's book of self-deliverance for the dying," by Derek Humphry, was published by the Hemlock Society in 1981 in the United States and reprinted every year since with an extensive revision in 1986. By relating actual stories of dying people who ended their lives, the book also includes precise drug dosages and other details.

In 1982, Editions Alain Moreau in Paris published *Suicide, Mode d'Emploi* (Suicide: Operating Methods), by Claude Guillon and Yves Le Bonniec. There were Japanese and German translations and the book had large sales in both countries. The book deals largely with suicide in French history and its political connotations. The drug dosage information is drawn from the publications of British EXIT, America's Hemlock, and the Dutch Voluntary Euthanasia Society.

In 1983, Anthos in the Netherlands published *Zorg jij dat ik niet meer wakker word?* (Will You See to It That I Don't Wake Up?) by Klazien Sybrandy and Rob Bakker. The book draws on Mrs. Sybrandy's extensive practical experience with assisted suicide for dying people. Lethal dosages and the manner in which they should be ingested are detailed.

At least five euthanasia societies have printed their own booklets detailing methods of self-deliverance but sell them only to members. They cannot be found in stores or libraries. The first was in 1980 by Scottish EXIT (now the Voluntary Euthanasia Society of Scotland), *How to Die with Dignity*, by Dr. George B. Mair, a retired physician. A revised edition is still sold to members. In 1981 British EXIT printed *A Guide to Self-Deliverance* (no specific author) and sold it to members only for a few months. After a court ruling that the book was liable to prosecution if used in connection with a suicide, EXIT stopped distribution. (English law says that not only is assisted suicide a crime but publications referring to it are also a felony.)

Autodeliverance (Self-deliverance) by Michel L. Landa, founder of *Association pour le Droit de Mourir dans la Dignité* in France, was published, in French only, in 1982, the year after Landa took his own life while suffering from lung cancer. The booklet is provided only to ADMD members. DGHS (Germany) and RWS (Belgium) have also produced self-deliverance handbooks for their members.

The only booklet written by a practicing physician on the subject is *Justifiable Euthanasia: A Manual for the Medical Profession*, by Pieter V. Admiraal, M.D., and printed by the Dutch Society for Voluntary Euthanasia in Amsterdam. Eleven pages long, it appeared in Dutch in 1983 and in English translation in 1984, and deals almost entirely with lethal drug dosages.

I am grateful to all the foregoing books and organizations for help with *Final Exit*.

—Derek Humphry

RECOMMENDED FURTHER READING

There are many fine books available today on dying and death. The following are the ones, by classification, that I believe could be the most helpful to readers of this book.

Case Histories

First You Cry, by Betty Rollin. (Signet, 1977)

Last Wish, by Betty Rollin. (Warner, 1987)

Death of a Man, by Lael Wertenbaker. (Random House, 1957)

Jean's Way, by Derek Humphry. (Dell, 1991)

History and Ethics

The Right to Die: Understanding Euthanasia, by Derek Humphry and Ann Wickett. (Hemlock Society, 1989)

Death by Choice, by Daniel C. Maguire. (Schocken Books, 1975)

Dying with Dignity, by Derek Humphry. (Carol Publishing, 1992)

Morals and Medicine, by Joseph Fletcher. (Beacon Press, 1954)

The Savage God: A Study of Suicide, by A. Alvarez. (Bantam Books, 1976)

Elder Suicide

Common Sense Suicide: The Final Right, by Doris Portwood. (Hemlock Society, 1980)

Compassionate Crimes, Broken Taboos, Derek Humphry, Editor. (Hemlock Society, 1980)

Double Exit: When Aging Couples Commit Suicide Together, by Ann Wickett. (Hemlock Society, 1988)

Religion

Euthanasia and Religion, by Gerald A. Larue. (Hemlock Society, 1985)

Bibliography

Voluntary Euthanasia: A Comprehensive Bibliography, Compiled by Gretchen Johnson. (Hemlock Society, 1988)

Law Reform

Death with Dignity: A New Law Permitting Physician Aid-in-Dying, by Robert L. Risley, J.D. (Hemlock Society, 1989)

Burial and Ceremonies

Dealing Creatively with Death: A Manual of Death Education and Simple Burial, by Ernest Morgan. Revised edition. (Celo Press, 1988). Available from the Hemlock Society.

Plays

Whose Life Is It Anyway? by Brian Clark. (Avon, 1980)

Is This the Day? by Vilma Hollingbery. (Hemlock Society, 1990)

Novels

Critical Care, by Richard Dooling. (Morrow, 1992)

The Woman Said Yes, by Jessamyn West. (Harcourt Brace Jovanovich, 1976)

In the Night Season, by Christiaan Barnard. (Prentice Hall, 1978)

Love Story, by Erich Segal. (Coronet, 1971)

Appendix A

The Death with Dignity Act
(Hemlock Society Model)
When Passed into Law

● Permits a competent terminally ill adult the right to request and receive physician aid-in-dying under carefully defined circumstances.

● Protects physicians from liability in carrying out a patient's request.

● Combines the concepts of Natural Death Acts and Durable Power of Attorney for Health Care laws, and makes them more usable.

● Permits a patient to appoint an attorney-in-fact to make health care decisions, including withholding and withdrawing life-support systems, and can empower the attorney-in-fact to decide about requesting aid-in-dying if the patient becomes incompetent.*

● Requires decision of the attorney-in-fact to be reviewed by a hospital ethics or other committee before the decision is acted upon by the physician.

● To take advantage of the law, a competent adult person must sign a Death with Dignity (DDA) directive.

*Aid-in-dying through a surrogate decision is not part of the Washington Initiative (1991) or the California Initiative (1992).

- Permits revocation of a directive at any time by any means.
- Requires hospitals and other health care facilities to keep records and report to the Department of Health Services after the death of the patient and then anonymously.
- Permits a treating physician to order a psychiatric consultation, with the patient's consent, if there is any question about the patient's competence to make the request for aid-in-dying.
- Forbids aid-in-dying to any patient solely because he or she is a burden to anyone, or because the patient is incompetent or terminal and has not made out an informed and proper (DDA) directive.
- Forbids aiding, abetting, and encouraging a suicide which remains a crime under the Act.
- Does not permit aid-in-dying to be administered by a loved one, family member, or stranger.
- Forbids aid-in-dying for children, incompetents, or anyone who has not voluntarily and intentionally completed and signed the properly witnessed (DDA) directive.
- Attempts to keep the decision-making process with the patient and health care provider, and out of court.
- Makes special protective provisions for patients in skilled nursing facilities.
- Permits doctors, nurses, and privately owned hospitals the right to decline a dying patient's request for aid-in-dying if they are morally or ethically opposed to such action.

Appendix B

Pain Control

• **American Chronic Pain Association,** Sacramento, Calif. (916) 632-0922. Self-help organization for pain patients, publishes workbook, teaches coping skills.

• **National Chronic Pain Outreach Association,** Bethesda, Md. (301) 652-4948. Information clearinghouse, makes referrals, publishes newsletters.

• **American Pain Society,** Skokie, Ill. (708) 966-5595. Professional organization of physicians and pain management experts. Makes referrals.

MULTIDISCIPLINARY CLINICS

This selective list names top programs based on similar philosophies of pain management, though some put slightly stronger emphasis on psychiatry or neurology.

• **Cleveland Clinic Foundation Research Institute** (216) 444-3900

• **Johns Hopkins Pain Management Service,** Baltimore (301) 955-1816

• **Mayo Clinic's Pain Management Center** at St. Mary's Hospital, Rochester, Minn. (507) 255-5921

- **Mensana Clinic,** Stevenson, Md. (410) 653-2403

- **New York Pain Treatment Program,** Lenox Hill Hospital, New York City (800) 548-3242

- **Pain Control & Rehabilitation Institute of Georgia,** Atlanta (404) 297-1400

- **University of Miami Comprehensive Pain & Rehabilitation Center** at Southshore Hospital, Miami (305) 672-3700

- **University of Washington Pain Center,** Seattle (206) 548-4282

CANCER CENTERS

These cancer care and research hospitals also have multimodality clinics devoted to pain management and quality of life.

- **Fred Hutchinson Cancer Research Center,** Seattle (206) 667-5000

- **Memorial Sloan-Kettering Cancer Center,** New York City (212) 639-2000

Appendix C

Suicide Hot Lines

Stop! Call! Talk!

If you are considering ending your life because of depression or inability to cope with life, please call one or more of the telephone numbers listed here. They may be able to help you to get through the crisis and return to normal existence.

American Association of Suicidology: (303) 692-0985. Available 9:00-5:00 MST, M-F. Provides information and referrals concerning suicide prevention. Also provides information for reports on suicide.

National Hotline for Young Persons: 1-800-621-4000

Statewide/County 800 Crisis Lines:

Alabama: 1-800-932-0501
Arkansas: 1-800-467-4673 and 1-800-825-6737
Arizona: 1-800-293-1749

California: 1-800-852-8336 and 1-800-444-9999
  San Diego County: 1-800-479-3339
  SLO County: 1-800-549-8989
Delaware: 1-800-345-6785, 1-800-262-9800, and
  1-800-652-2929
Florida
  Monroe County: 1-800-228-5463
Illinois: 1-800-638-4357
  McLean County: 1-800-322-5015
Indiana: 1-800-832-5378, 1-800-552-3106, and
  1-800-537-1302
Iowa: 1-800-638-4357 and 1-800-356-9588
Kentucky: 1-800-562-8909, 1-800-262-7491,
  1-800-221-0446, 1-800-822-5902, 1-800-592-
  3980, and 1-800-422-1060
Maine: 1-800-431-7810, 1-800-452-1933, and
  1-800-432-7805
Maryland: 1-800-422-0009 and 1-800-540-5806
Michigan: 1-800-322-0444 and 1-800-442-7315
  (313) only: 1-800-462-6350
Minnesota: 1-800-356-9588, 1-800-462-5525, and
  1-800-223-4512
Missouri: 1-800-223-5176
Nevada: 1-800-992-5757
Nebraska: 1-800-638-4357
New Hampshire: 1-800-852-3323 and 1-800-852-
  3388
New Mexico: 1-800-432-2159
New York
  Wayne County: 1-800-333-0542
North Carolina: 1-800-672-2903

North Dakota: 1-800-638-4357 and 1-800-471-2911
Ohio: 1-800-523-4146
  Wood County: 1-800-872-9411
  Portage County: 1-800-533-4357
  Lawrence County: 1-800-448-2273
Oklahoma: 1-800-522-8336
Oregon: 1-800-452-3669
Rhode Island: 1-800-365-4044
South Carolina: 1-800-922-2283
South Dakota: 1-800-638-4357
Texas: 1-800-692-4039
Utah: 1-800-626-8399
Virginia: 1-800-768-2273 and 1-800-251-7596
Washington: 1-800-244-7414 and 1-800-572-8122
Wisconsin: 1-800-362-8255 and 1-800-638-4357

OR:

Consult the Yellow Pages under "Hot Lines" or "Crisis Intervention."

Appendix D

A Living Will and Durable Power of Attorney for Health Care

Plus Guide to Completion

To my family, my friends, my doctors and all those concerned: Directive made this _____ day of _____, 19__.

I, _____ (name), being an adult of sound mind, willfully and voluntarily make this directive to be followed if I become incapable of participating in decisions regarding my medical treatment.

1. If at any time I should have an incurable or irreversible condition certified to be terminal by two medical doctors who have examined me, one of whom is my attending physician, or when use of life-sustaining treatment would only serve to artificially prolong the moment of my death, I direct that the expression of my intent be followed and that my dying not be prolonged. I further direct that I receive treatment necessary to keep me comfortable and to relieve pain.

INITIAL ONE:

____ I would like life-sustaining treatment, including artificial nutrition and hydration, to be withdrawn or withheld.

____ I would like life-sustaining treatment withdrawn or

186

withheld, but artificial nutrition and hydration continued.

Additional Instructions[1]: _____

_____

2. I appoint _____, residing at
_____, as my agent, to
make medical treatment decisions on my behalf, consistent
with this directive.

3. If I have been diagnosed as pregnant and that diagnosis is
known to my physician, this directive shall not be effective
during the course of my pregnancy.[2]

4. This directive shall have no force and effect after __ years
from the date of its execution, nor, if sooner, after revocation
by me either orally or in writing.[3]

5. I understand the full importance of this directive and am
emotionally and mentally competent to make this living will.

Signed _____

City, County, and State of Residence _____

**Caution: Check the numbered footnotes. Some provisions
may not apply to you.**

WITNESSES TO LIVING WILL

The declarant is personally known to me and I believe her/him
to be at an adult and of sound mind.

I am not[4]:

1. Related to the declarant by blood or marriage;
2. Entitled to any portion of the declarant's estate either by will
or codicil, or according to the laws of intestate succession;

187

3. Directly financially responsible for the declarant's medical care;
4. The declarant's doctor or an employee of that doctor;
5. An employee or patient in the hospital where the declarant is a patient.

_____   _____
Witness   Address

_____   _____
Witness   Address

NOTARIZATION[5]

State of _____)
) ss.
County of _____)
  Subscribed and sworn to before me by _____
_____, Declarant and
_____, wit-
nesses, as the voluntary act and deed of the declarant this
_____ day of _____, 19__.
My commission expires:

_____
Notary Public

NOTES

1. Include any related expressions of your intent; for example, organ donation, that you wish to die at home, specific types of treatment you do not want, such as cardiopulmonary resuscitation (CPR) or antibiotics, etc.

2. Many states have provisions in their Living Will statutes regarding pregnancy. If you do not desire this provision in your Living Will, draw a line through that part of the directive and

initial it, keeping in mind that in the event of pregnancy, states with such a provision may enforce it.

3. Some states limit the time for which a directive is valid. If this does not apply to you and you wish your directive not to expire, draw a line through that part of the directive and initial it.

4. Because many of the states with Living Will statutes contain all or some of these restrictions, we recommend that you choose witnesses who are not in any of these categories. If you are a resident of Georgia, a third witness is required when the directive is signed in the hospital. If you are in a nursing home, we suggest that one witness be a patient advocate or ombudsperson.

5. Notarization, in addition to witnessing, is required in the following states: Hawaii, New Hampshire, North Carolina, Oklahoma, South Carolina, and West Virginia. It is suggested by the statutes in Colorado and Tennessee. Alaska and Minnesota allow *either* signature by two witnesses *or* notarization.

DURABLE POWER OF ATTORNEY FOR HEALTH CARE

NOTICE: This document gives the person you name as your attorney-in-fact the power to make health care decisions for you only if you cannot make the decision for yourself. This includes the right to see your medical records.

After you have signed this document, you have the right to make the health care decisions for yourself if you are capable of doing so. You also have the right to prevent treatment from being given to you or from being stopped.

You may state in this document any type of treatment that you do not desire or that you want to make sure you receive.

You have the right to revoke the authority of your attorney-in-fact, either orally or in writing. If you do take away that authority, notify everyone with a copy of the Power of Attorney, ideally in writing.

If there is anything in this document that you do not understand, ask your lawyer to explain it to you.

You should keep a copy of this document after you have signed it. Give a copy to the person(s) you name as your attorney-in-fact and alternate. Give copies to your regular doctors and any health care facility where you have been and expect to be a patient again.

Creation of Durable Power of Attorney. By this document I intend to create a Durable Power of Attorney for Health Care. This power of attorney shall not be affected by my subsequent incapacity or disability.

Revocation. I revoke any prior Durable Power of Attorney for Health Care.

Designation of Attorney-in-fact and Alternate. I appoint _____, whose address is _____, and whose telephone number is _____, as my attorney-in-fact for health care decisions. I appoint _____, whose address is _____, and whose telephone number is _____, as my alternative attorney-in-fact for health care decisions. I authorize my attorney-in-fact appointed by this document to make health care decisions for me when I am incapable of making my own health care decisions.

Desires, Special Instructions, Limitations[1]:_____

_____

In addition, I direct that my attorney-in-fact have authority to make decisions regarding the following:
(INITIAL ONE OR BOTH.)

__ Withholding or withdrawal of life-sustaining procedures with the understanding that death may result.

__ Withholding or withdrawal of artificially administered hydration or nutrition or both with the understanding that death may result.

I understand the contents of this document and the powers granted to my attorney-in-fact.

Signed_____ Date_____

WITNESSES TO THE DURABLE POWER OF ATTORNEY FOR HEALTH CARE[2]

The declarant is personally known to me and I believe her/him to be at least 18 years old, and of sound mind. I am not:

1. Related to the declarant by blood or marriage;
2. Entitled to any portion of the declarant's estate either by will or codicil, or according to the laws of intestate succession;
3. Directly financially responsible for the declarant's medical care;
4. The declarant's doctor or an employee of that doctor;
5. An employee or patient in the hospital or health care facility where the declarant is a patient.

_____   _____

Witness   Address

_____   _____

Witness   Address

Caution: Check the numbered footnotes. Some provisions may not apply to you.

NOTARIZATION[3]

State of _____)
) ss.
County of _____)

Subscribed and sworn to before me by _____
_____, Declarant and
_____, wit-
nesses, as the voluntary act and deed of the declarant this
_____ day of _____, 19__.

My commission expires:

_____
Notary Public

ACCEPTANCE OF APPOINTMENT OF POWER OF ATTORNEY[4]

I have discussed with _____
(principal) and agree to serve as attorney-in-fact for health care
decisions. I understand I have a duty to act consistently with the
desires of the principal as expressed in this appointment. I understand that this document gives me authority over health care
decisions for the principal only if the principal becomes incapable or otherwise disabled. I understand that I must act in good
faith in exercising my authority under this power of attorney. I
understand that the principal may revoke this power of attorney
at any time in any manner.

_____   _____
Signature of Attorney-in-fact   Date

_____   _____
Signature of Alternate Attorney-in-fact   Date

192

Caution: Check the numbered notes. Some provisions may not apply to you.

1. Use this space to note the types of treatment you want done or do not want done; some examples are CPR, antibiotics, respirators, organ donation, transfusions. You may add additional pages of instructions; be sure to sign and date them.

2. Although witnesses are not required in several states, and the requirements of who may be a witness vary from state to state, we recommend that you have your Durable Power of Attorney for Health Care witnessed according to this form. This may help protect you if you move to or become disabled in another state. Your attorney-in-fact and alternate should *never* be witnesses.

3. Notarization, in addition to witnessing, is required in Illinois. Maine, New Jersey, and Utah require only notarization. Nevada, California, and Idaho allow *either* signature by two witnesses *or* notarization. We recommend notarization of this form, when possible, even if you do not live in one of the specified states.

4. New Jersey and Oregon require a signed acceptance by the attorney-in-fact. New York requires a statement of discussion. We recommend that you discuss your desires with your attorney-in-fact and have him or her sign this acceptance.

COMMON QUESTIONS ABOUT THE LIVING WILL

1. What is a Living Will?

A Living Will (often called a Medical Directive or Directive to Physicians) is a document which lets you tell your doctor in advance that you do not want your life artificially extended in

193

certain situations. The two situations where a directive may be used are (1) when you have an incurable injury, disease, or illness which two doctors agree is terminal; and (2) when life-sustaining procedures would only prolong the moment of your death, when you would die whether these procedures were used or not.

2. Who can make a Living Will?

You must be at least 18 years of age or older, and of sound mind to make a Living Will in most states.

3. Who can witness a Living Will?

A majority of states require that only certain people witness a Living Will. At the time the Living Will is witnessed, the witnesses should not be related to you by blood or marriage, entitled to part of your estate if you die, either through your will, by law, or because of bills owed, or be your attending doctor or an employee of that doctor or the health care facility where you are a patient.

4. If I make a Living Will, is it permanent?

A Living Will is permanent from the time it is finalized, except in California and North Dakota. If you change your mind at any time, you may revoke the directive by destroying it, writing down your intent or telling someone. Make sure to tell your doctor and anyone else with a copy of the directive of changes.

5. What if my doctor doesn't want to honor my Living Will?

A doctor who doesn't want to honor a Living Will is required by most laws to try to find another doctor or health care facility where your wishes will be carried out. Talk with your doctor when you complete your Living Will, giving him or her a copy for your medical record, so you can be sure that you agree.

6. Will completing a Living Will affect my insurance policies?

No. Most statutes specify that insurance policies will not be legally impaired or invalidated by signing a directive or putting it into effect.

7. Where should I keep my Living Will?

Keep your original Living Will in a safe place in your home, give a photocopy to a friend or family member, and be sure to give a photocopy to your doctor for his or her record and a hospital where you have a medical record and would go when hospitalized.

8. Is my Living Will legally enforceable?

No. While it is recognized by law in most states, health care providers are not always required to comply with it. It is a request and of value as evidence. Most doctors will respect a Living Will as a lawful refusal of treatment.

COMMON QUESTIONS ABOUT THE DURABLE POWER OF ATTORNEY FOR HEALTH CARE

1. What is a Durable Power of Attorney for Health Care?

A Durable Power of Attorney for Health Care lets you choose a person in advance to make medical or health care decisions for you if you become incapable of doing so.

2. Who can make such a power of attorney?

A person who is an adult and has the capacity to make health care decisions may make a power of attorney.

3. Do I need a lawyer to write a Power of Attorney for Health Care?

Although you do not need a lawyer to write a Power of Attorney for Health Care, if there is anything in the document that you do not understand, you should consult a lawyer.

4. Who will decide that I am incapable of making my own health care decisions?

Usually your attending doctor and one other doctor determine that you are not capable of making health care decisions; in rare cases a court will decide.

5. How long does a Power of Attorney for Health Care last?

The period of time for which a Power of Attorney for Health Care is good may vary by state. It may also end if you die, if you revoke it, or if both the attorney-in-fact and alternate attorney-in-fact withdraw. If you become incapable of making health care decisions during the period of validity and the power of attorney goes into effect, it will remain in effect until you are no longer incapable or until you die.

You should periodically review both your Living Will and power of attorney, revising them when necessary.

6. What if I change my mind?

If you change your mind at any time about who should be your attorney-in-fact, what decisions he or she may make, or whether you want a Power of Attorney for Health Care, you can revoke the power of attorney in any manner. Make sure that you let your doctor and anyone with copies know that you have changed your mind.

7. Who can be my attorney-in-fact?

An attorney-in-fact does not have to be a lawyer; he or she can be any adult you choose except for your attending doctor or an employee of that doctor who is not related to you by blood, marriage, or adoption; or an owner, operator, or employee of a health care facility where you are a patient or resident, if they are not related to you by blood, marriage, or adoption.

The person you choose should agree in writing to serve as your attorney-in-fact; he or she can withdraw at any time.

If you choose your husband or wife as attorney-in-fact and later divorce, you will need to make a new power of attorney naming that person or someone else as attorney-in-fact.

8. What kinds of decisions will my attorney-in-fact be able to make?

A written Power of Attorney for Health Care gives only the authority to make health care decisions for you that you would have made if you were not incapable. If you want that person to make decisions about withdrawing or withholding a procedure or food and water necessary to keep you alive, you should say so on the power of attorney. Your attorney-in-fact will also have a right to see your medical records.

Your attorney-in-fact must act according to what he or she believes that you would want, or if that is not known, in your best interest.

9. What if my doctor doesn't want to honor the wishes of my attorney-in-fact?

A doctor who fails to honor your wishes regarding consent to or refusal of treatment may be liable for damages, because you have a common law and constitutional right to make such decisions. Talk to your doctor when you complete your Durable

Power of Attorney for Health Care, giving him or her a copy for your medical record, so you can be sure you agree.

10. Will my attorney-in-fact be responsible for the cost of my medical care?

No. Your attorney-in-fact is acting in a decision-making capacity and is only responsible for making health care decisions.

ABOUT THE AUTHOR

Born in Bath, England, in 1930, Derek Humphry left school at 15 and entered journalism as a messenger boy. At 16 he was a junior reporter on the *Bristol Evening World.* He became a journalist first on the *Manchester Evening News* and then the London *Daily Mail.* At 33 he became editor of the *Havering Recorder,* a London suburban newspaper, moving to the London *Sunday Times* five years later.

In 1971 he published *Because They're Black,* a book explaining the lives of black people to white people, which won the Martin Luther King Memorial Prize for its contribution to racial harmony in Britain. He followed this with other books on race, civil liberties and a biography of Michael X, the black power leader in Britain.

After ten years as a *Sunday Times* correspondent, he emigrated in 1978 to America to work for the *Los Angeles Times* as a special writer. The international acceptance of *Jean's Way,* the story of his helping his first wife to die when her cancer became unbearable to her, launched him into a career in the voluntary euthanasia movement through the Hemlock Society, of which he was the principal founder.

His other books are *Let Me Die Before I Wake,*

The Right to Die: Understanding Euthanasia and *Dying with Dignity.* He lives in the hills above Eugene, Oregon, with sailing as his hobby.

He was executive director of the Hemlock Society from 1980 to 1992, and from 1988 to 1990 was president of the World Federation of Right to Die Societies.

ABOUT THE HEMLOCK SOCIETY

Motto: "Good Life, Good Death"

Formed in 1980 in Los Angeles to campaign for the right of a terminally ill person to choose voluntary euthanasia, the Hemlock Society has grown steadily to a membership of 57,000 after twelve years. It has eighty-six chapters.

Although the principal founder, Derek Humphry, is English, Hemlock is a wholly American organization, incorporated under California and Oregon laws, with an IRS nonprofit tax status of 501(c)(3). The other founders of Hemlock were Ann Wickett, Gerald A. Larue, and Richard S. Scott.

Hemlock publishes newsletters and books, holds conferences, conducts research, makes educational videos, and calls public meetings, all with the intention of raising consciousness about the right of terminally ill persons to choose to die in a manner of their choice.

Sister groups of Hemlock have made attempts to change the law. Americans Against Human Suffering launched an initiative (referendum) reform in California in 1988 but failed through weak organization to gather sufficient signatures. They are making a second attempt in 1992.

Hemlock of Washington State qualified an initiative to the legislature for an electoral vote in November 1991. It failed 54 percent to 46 percent. Legislative campaigns to reform the law are planned for Oregon and Florida.

The aim of these groups is to have *The Death with Dignity Act*, which would permit physician aid-in-dying for the terminally ill, passed into law.

Membership in the National Hemlock Society costs $25 a year ($35 for a couple) with a senior citizen discount of $5 on each fee. Life membership is $250 single and $300 for a couple. Free information from:

Hemlock Society
PO Box 11830
Eugene, OR 97440-4030

Telephone: (503) 342-5748

To obtain a combined Living Will and Durable Power of Attorney for Health Care, send your name and address with $3.50 to the above address. (These advance directives come free with membership in the Hemlock Society.)

INDEX

Autopsy, 69–73, 112
air embolism detection, 34–35
benefits, 71
legal status, 69–70

Ballade of Suicide, A (Chesterton), 100
Barbiturates, 84–85, 88, 93, 128, 168
combined use of, 127, 128, 170, 171–172
tolerance for, 172
see also specific names
Battery, 81
Belgium, drug names, 122
Bettelheim, Bruno, xx
Black market, 85
Bouvia, Elizabeth, 48–49
Brallobarbital, 108, 125
Brazil, drug purchase in, 84
Brewer, Colin, 35, 92–93
Britain. *see* EXIT; Great Britain
Buck, Gerald, 66–68
Buddhism, 72
Bulgaria, autopsy in, 69–70
Burotto, Abbie, 34
Butabarbital, 120
Butisol. *see* Butabarbital

California
euthanasia in, 142–143, 153
force feeding illegality, 48
hospices, 21
penalty for assisted suicide, xix, 146
Campbell, Steven Paul, 145–146
Canada, drug names, 122, 124, 125
Cancer, 57, 58
Carbrital. *see* Pentobarbital
Carothers, Wallace, 23
Cars
accidents, 38

exhaust gassing, 41
Cessation of treatment. *see* Passive Euthanasia
Chemists, 25
Chemotherapy, 58
Chesterton, G.K., 100
Chevalier, Maurice, 102
Chloral hydrate, 122
Chloratex. *see* Chloral hydrate
Civil law. *see* Legal system
Cleaners and chemicals, 42, 109
Codeine, 108, 120
Colorado, suicide and life insurance law, 66–67
Coma
cyanide-induced, 28, 51
drug-produced, 160, 172
from self-starvation, 53
Coming Home (movie), 33
Compazine, *see* Prochlorperazine
Containers
as intent evidence, 112
for lethal drugs, 60–61
Convulsions, 28
Coppens, Myriam, 141
Criminal law. *see* Legal system
Crisis Intervention Center, 129
Cruzan, Nancy, 6, 65
Curare, 172
Cyanide, 23–32
drawbacks of, 129
effectiveness of, 25, 30
effects of, 28, 30, 31–32
forms of, 27–28
lethal dosage, 28
obtaining, 32
painful effects of, 24, 26, 27, 32, 129
recommended technique, 31

Dalmadorm. *see* Flurazepam
Dalmane (flurazepam), 87, 122, 130, 146
Darvocet. *see* Propoxyphene

Ethics issues *(cont.)*
  and hospice choice, 20–21
  and physician-assisted
    euthanasia, 139, 155–156
Ethnor. *see* Butabarbital
Eunoctal. *see* Amobarbital
Europe. *see* specific country names
Euthanasia
  basic types, 162–163
  best site for, 156–157
  direct, 169
  drugs for physician-assisted,
    157–161
  fear of pain link, 21
  in Germany, 29–32
  and handicapped, 46–51
  intravenous, 171–172
  legal status, xxi, 155, 163
  medical profession involvement,
    133–172
  nurse-assisted, 162–165
  options, 3–7, 48–50
  oral, 169–171
  physician-assisted, 154–161
  physicians' viewpoints, 8–12
  in practice, 166–172
  prescription, 167–169
  and quality of life, xviii, 22, 49–
    50, 102–103, 135–139
  rational vs. nonrational, 104–
    106
  and religious beliefs, 4
  timing of, 155
  see also Active euthanasia;
    Assisted suicide; Suicide
Executions, 26–27
EXIT (British group), 16, 47

Family
  and Alzheimer's disease, 151
  and autoeuthanasia intent, 63–
    64, 81–83, 100–102, 116
  autopsy consent, 70

  and euthanasia decision, 154–
    155
  and hospice care, 19, 20
  joint suicide, 96–99
  as passive euthanasia surrogate,
    5–6
  and privacy protection, 75–77
  traumatic suicides and, 109
Federman, Daniel D., 139
Felony, 4
Fenical. *see* Phenobarbital
Fiction, 33, 56
Fletcher, Joseph, 97
Florida
  assisted suicide case, 105–106
  terminally ill list, 73
Flurazepam, 122
Food
  barbiturates mixed with, 170
  drug absorption and, 110, 111,
    117
  force feeding, 48, 54
  poison and empty stomach, 28
  self-starvation, 48, 52–54
Food and Drug Administration,
  U.S., 59, 61–62
Foxglove, 42
France
  autopsy in, 70
  drug names, 120, 125
  euthanasia status in, xxi
  hospice care, 19
Freezer, contraindication for
  lethal drugs, 60
Freezing, 43–44
Friends, informing of suicide
  intent, 63–64, 81–83, 116
Fruit seeds, 27

Gardenal. *see* Phenobarbital
Gassing, 41
Gehrig's disease. *see* Amyotrophic
  Lateral Sclerosis
Geriatrics. *see* Terminal old age

206

212

CASUALTIES OF AGE

Why do so many of our elders
commit suicide?

An investigation by
Derek Humphry

If you would like to assist the author in this
ground-breaking study of the reasons why so
many senior citizens choose to end their lives,
or consider doing so, please write to him:

Derek Humphry
Casualties of Age
P.O. Box 10603
Eugene, OR 97440-2603

Needed are:

- Case histories

- Personal experiences

- Well-argued views for and against

- Hitherto unrevealed data